ALAN GOVENAR

THE RETABLOS OF JERONIMO LOZANO

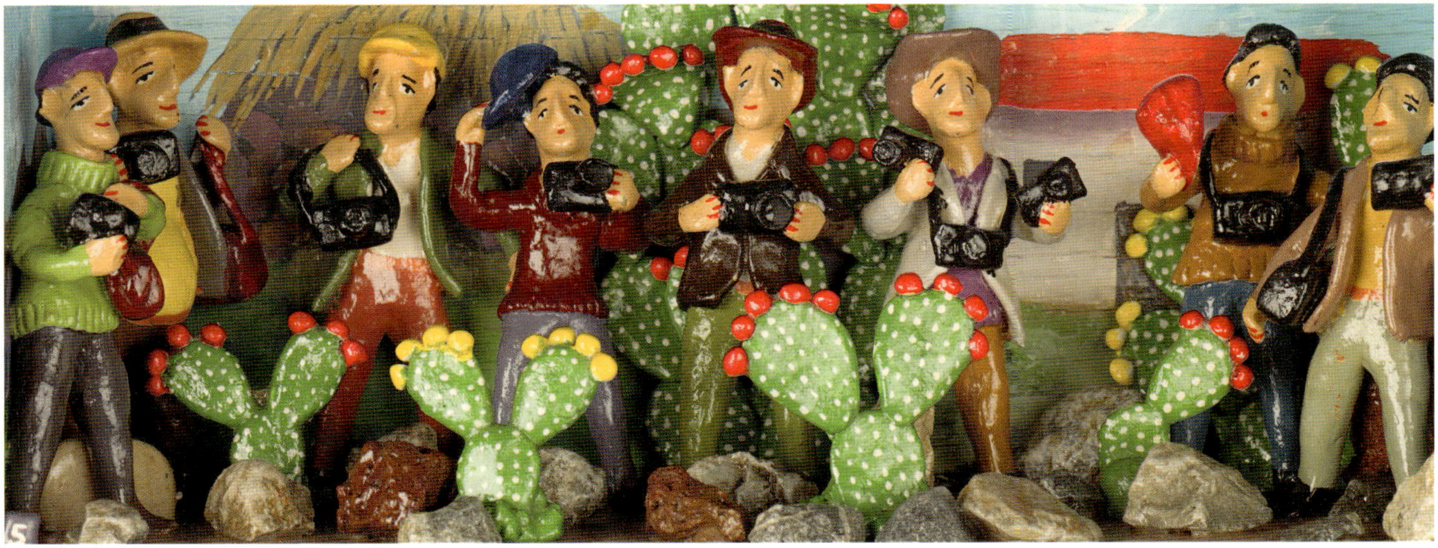

FROM PERU TO UTAH

SCHIFFER PUBLISHING
4880 Lower Valley Road • Atglen, PA 19310

Other Schiffer Books by the Author:
Stoney Knows How: Life as a Sideshow Tatoo Artist,
ISBN 978-0-7643-6400-6
The Early Years of Rhythm & Blues,
ISBN 978-0-7643-1983-9

Library of Congress Control Number: 2022932676

Cover design by Brenda McCallum
Cover Retablo by Jeronimo Lozano; Photo by Kevin Todora
Type set in Fink/ Universe

ISBN: 978-0-7643-6520-1
Printed in India

Published by Schiffer Publishing, Ltd.
4880 Lower Valley Road
Atglen, PA 19310
Phone: (610) 593-1777; Fax: (610) 593-2002
Email: Info@schifferbooks.com
Web: www.schifferbooks.com

Photographs and edited interviews by Alan Govenar

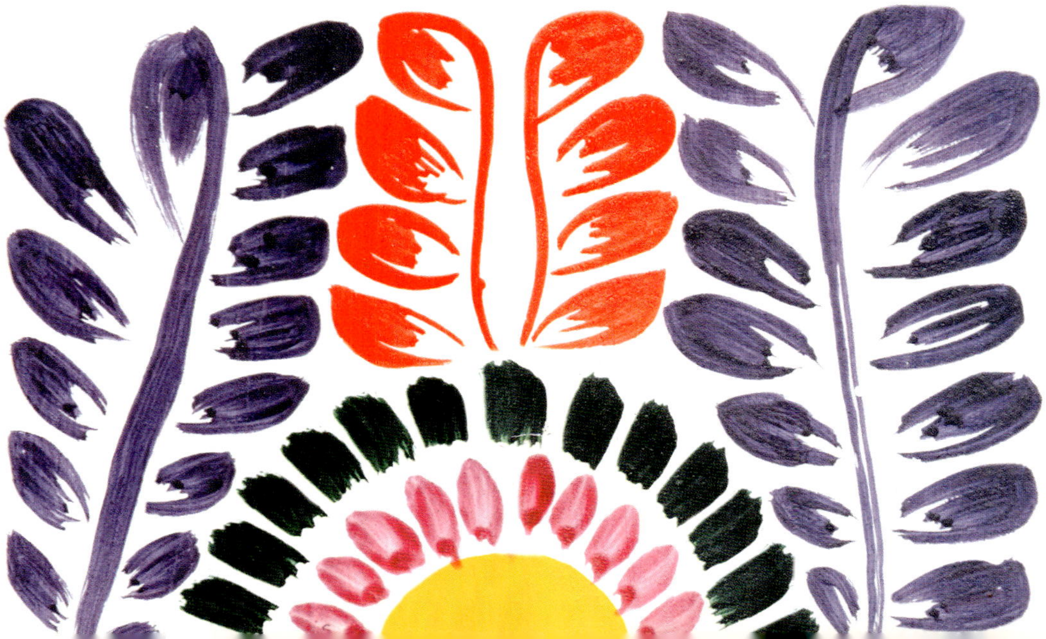

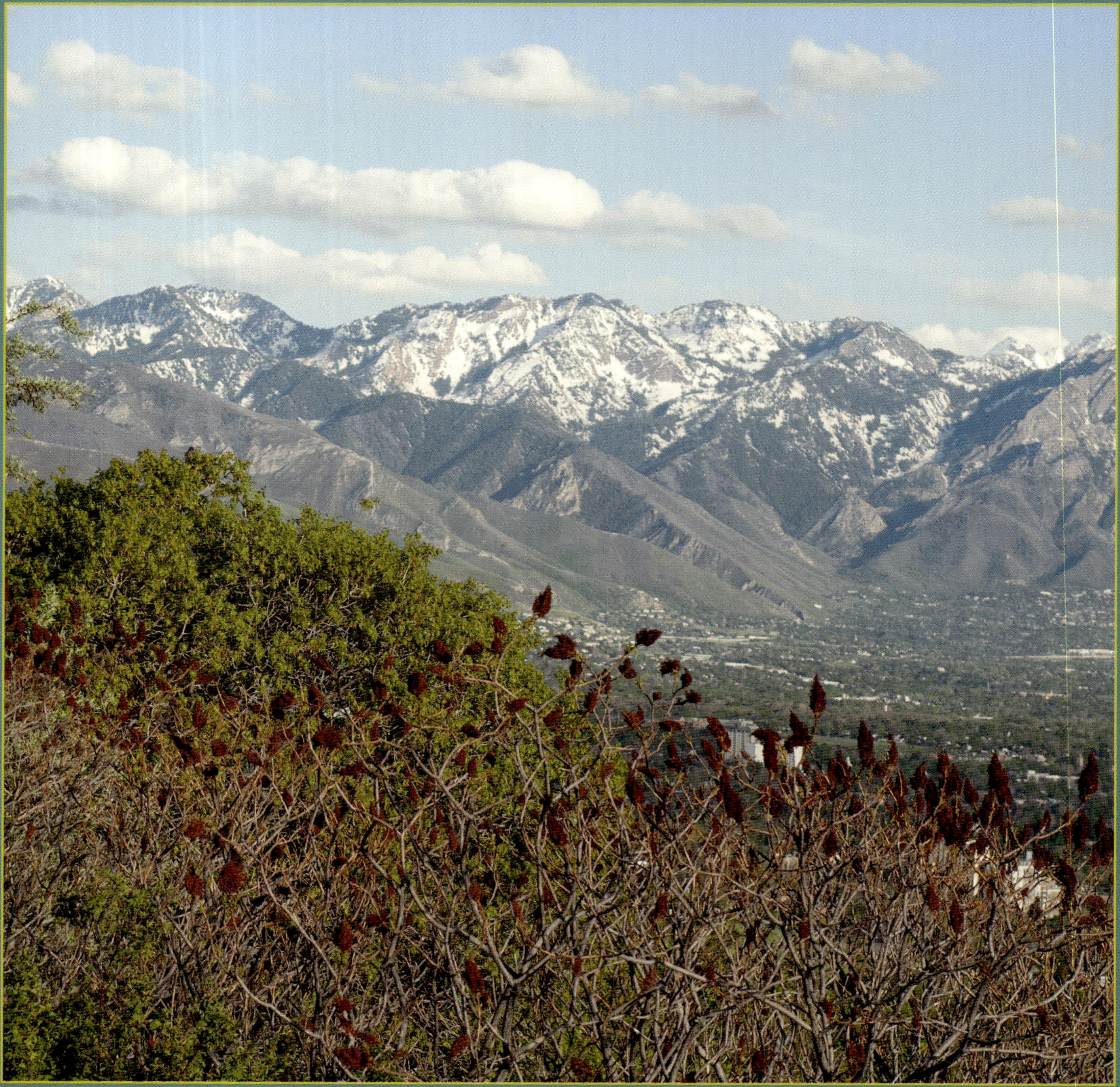

Introduction

Flying to Utah, the light has a clarity that intensifies the quiet drama of the Wasatch Mountains to the east and north, and the Oquirrh Mountains to the west. Descending through the high cumulus clouds hovering over the snow-capped peaks, the valley spreads out before me, and I start to think of the villages in the Andes where Jeronimo Lozano was born and raised. Once on the ground, the air is crisp; the sky, sapphire blue; and the reality of Salt Lake City comes into view.

On my way to Jeronimo's apartment, I pass a sign for the City Creek Inn that makes me smile to myself about clichés of the American West and the apocryphal founding of Salt Lake City by the Mormon Brigham Young and the rapid growth of the Church of Jesus Christ of Latter-day Saints.

Jeronimo's face glows as he invites me into his apartment. I feel as if I'm entering a fantasy world, surrounded by hand-painted figures and intricately crafted retablos that are at once whimsical and devotional. It is evident that his faith is primary in his life, but he has a playfulness that belies his age.

Born July 20, 1950, Jeronimo Lozano dedicated his life to the ancient Peruvian tradition of handcrafted retablos. Originally made as portable altar boxes, retablos were carried by travelers for protection. The Spaniards brought retablos to Peru, and in them, they placed images and small sculpted figures of Catholic saints that likely derive from the painted diptychs found in medieval European churches. While many of Jeronimo's retablos have Christian themes, his work also includes secular scenes with historical and current references, from everyday life in the villages of the Ayacucho region of Peru to political commentary, from circus performers to shopkeepers in their market stands, and from street processions to fiestas.

Jeronimo came to the United States in 1994, while on a tour of the United States with a folkloric dance troupe, and applied for an extended visa to flee the growing terrorism in Peru. With the help of Kirk Henrichsen and other members of the Church of Jesus Christ of Latter-day Saints, he was able to settle in Salt Lake City. In 2002, he was recognized with the Utah Governor's Folk Art Award, and in 2008, he received a National Heritage Fellowship from the National Endowment for the Arts.

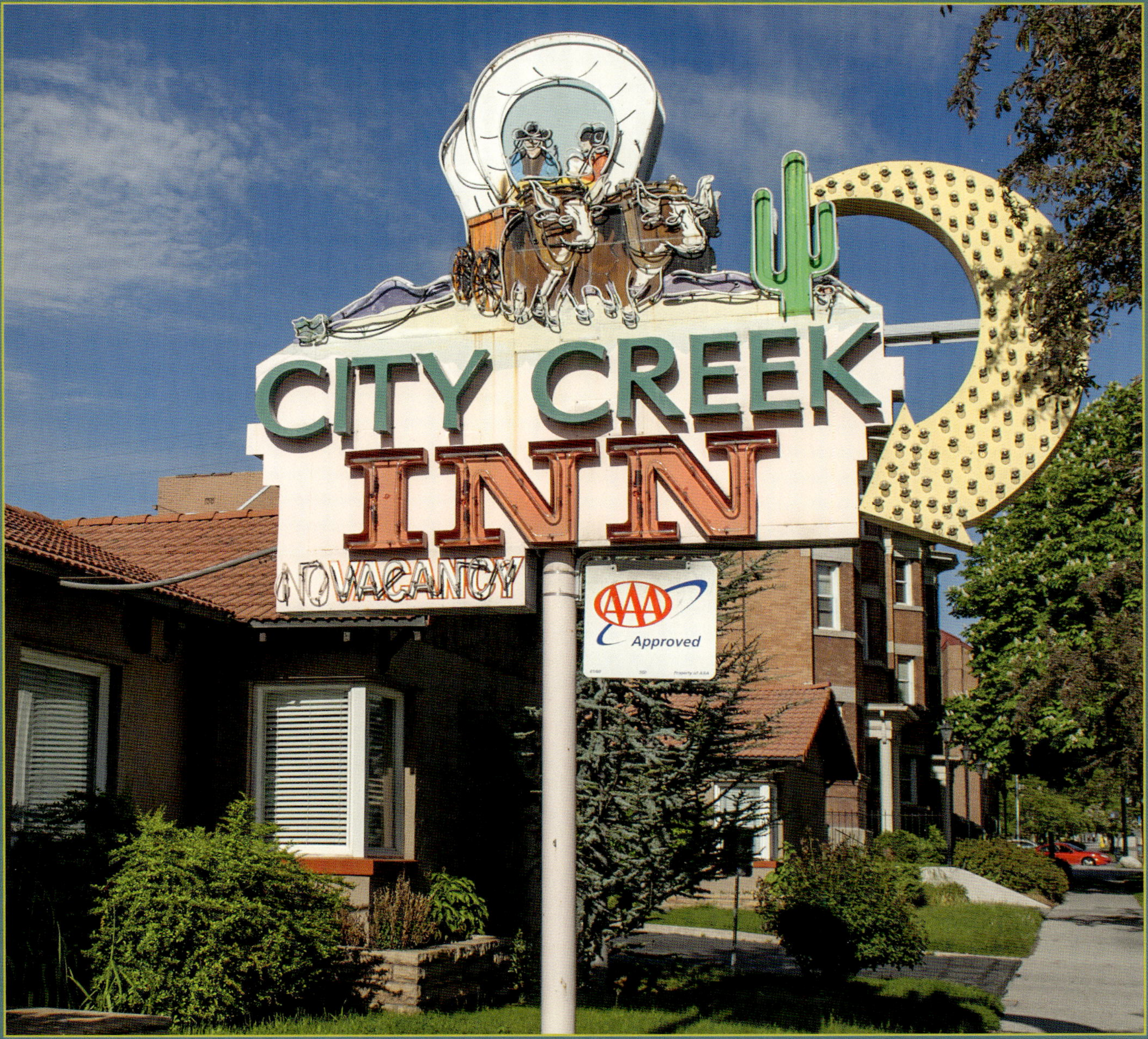
CITY CREEK
INN
NO VACANCY
AAA
Approved

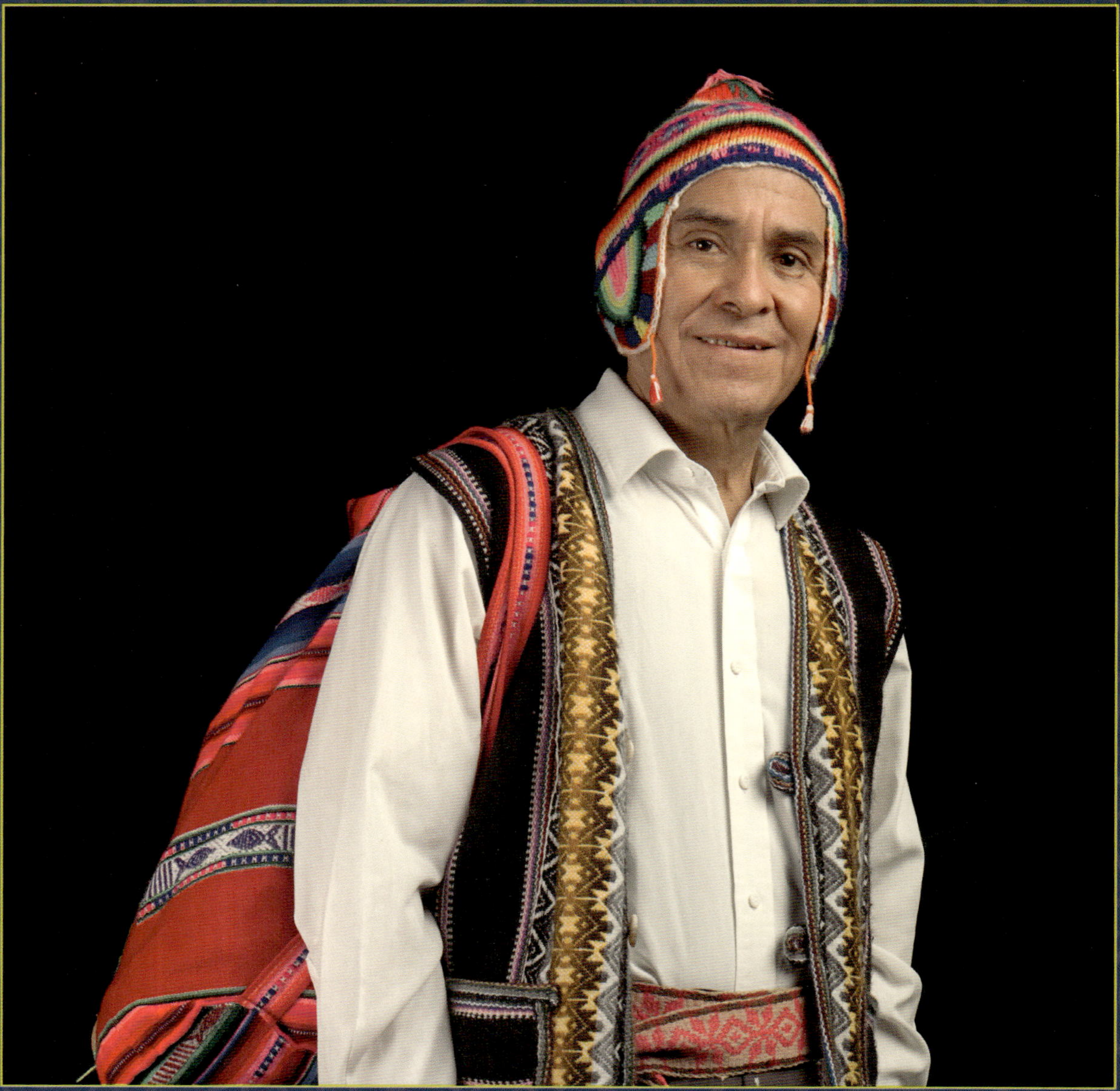

My Story

I grew up in Ayacucho, in the high mountains of Peru. We lived in a village named Rancha. That community was very small, maybe 150 people. Most of the families had my last name, Lozano. My parents worked in agriculture. They grew corn, wheat, potatoes, beans. We had a few animals: bulls, lambs, chickens. And we had donkeys and a dog and cats. We had little money. So, what we couldn't buy we traded for, exchanging what we had grown or did for other kinds of products that other people had. We survived.

I began modeling clay when I was about six or seven years old. I saw white clay sand models and noticed clays made from plaster and chalk. So, at home, I wanted to see the difference. When my mom cooked potatoes, I held some back after eating and mixed some of the potatoes with chalk and some with plaster. I modeled people with the chalk mix, and animals with plaster, and let them dry. After a while, when I held the chalk model figures, they broke, and the plaster didn't. So I chose plaster for the figures in my retablos.

When I walked in the mountains, I saw the people who lived there and saw the retablos they had. Once, I met a woman who brought me a retablo of hers, so that I could repair the figures that were broken. And when she left me with that retablo, I was so impressed, because it was the first time that I had seen such an intricate retablo, but I had no idea who made it.

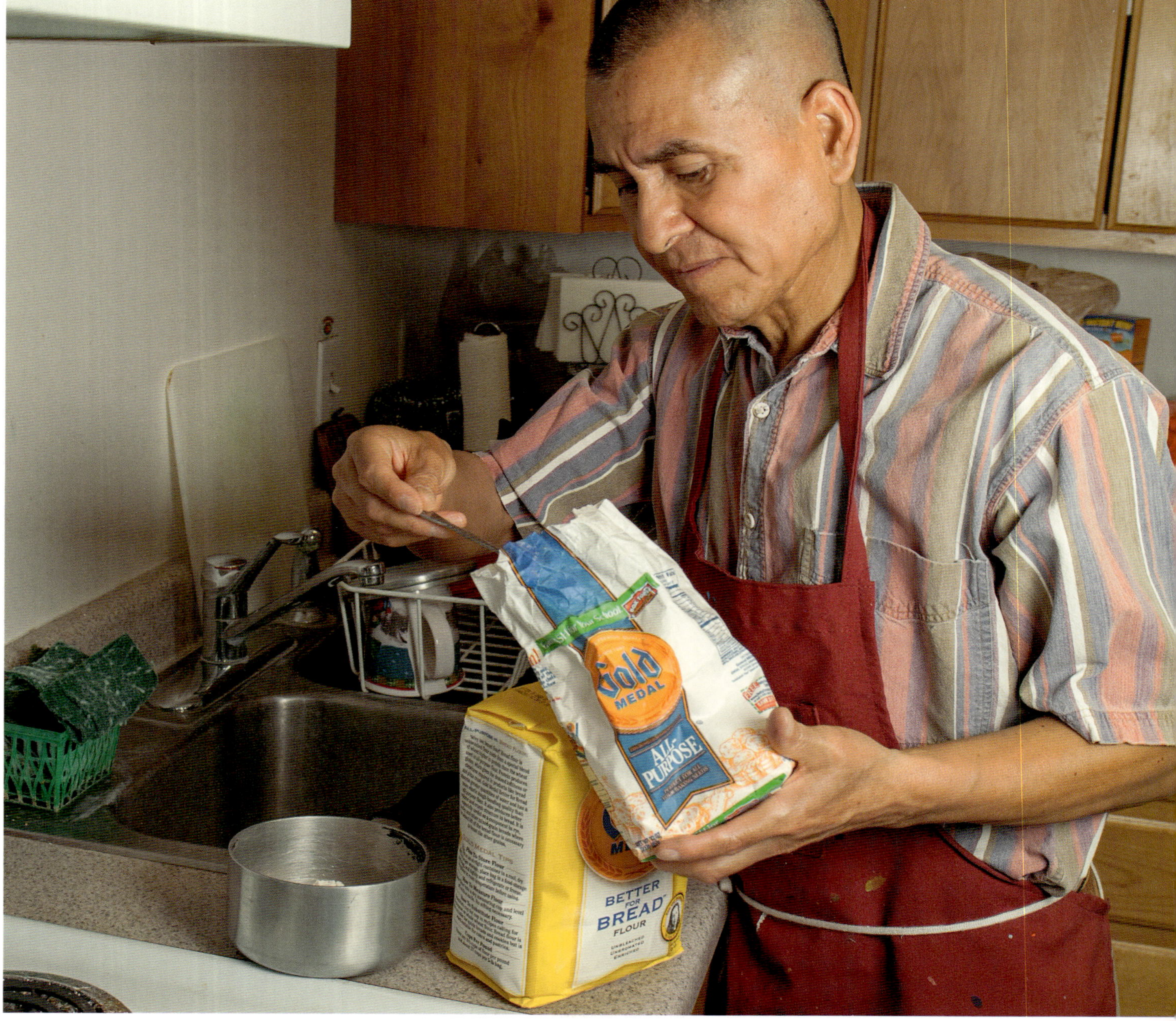
Gold
MEDAL
ALL-PURPOSE
BETTER FOR BREAD FLOUR

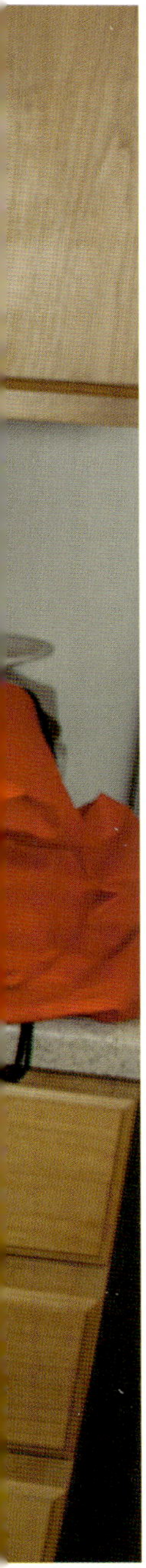

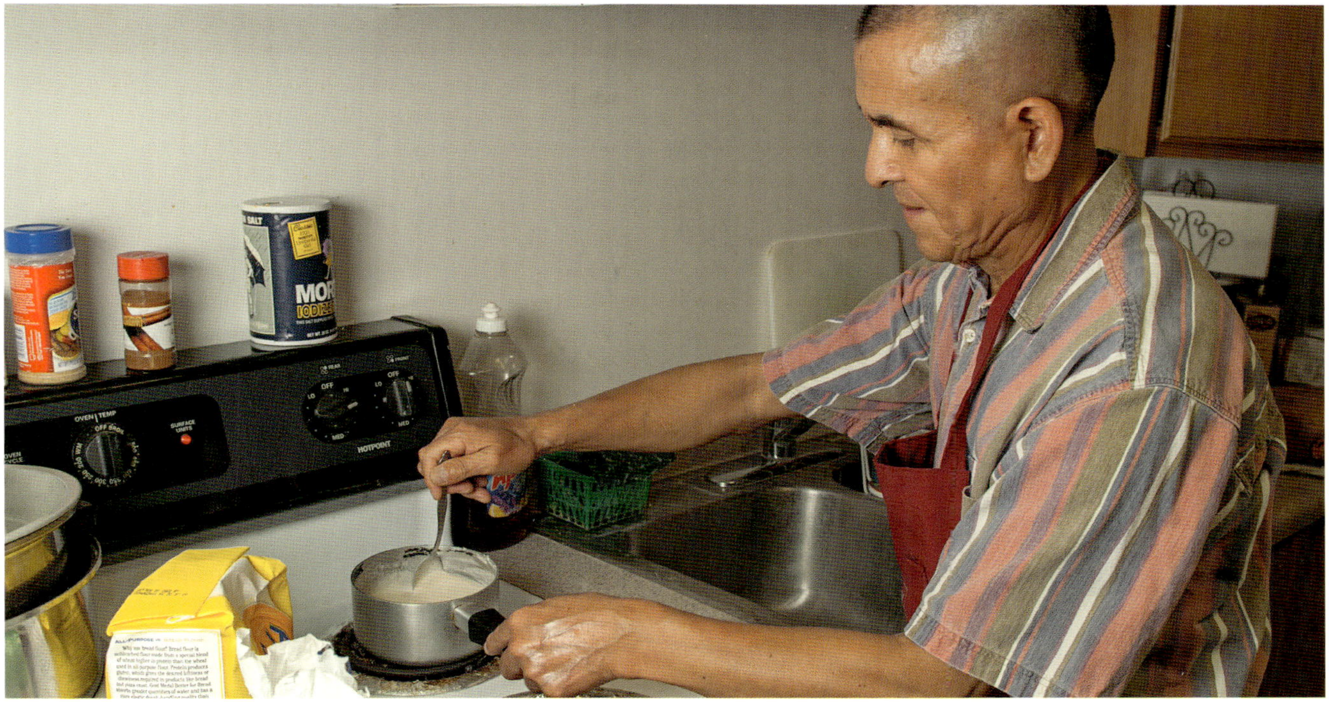
HOTPOINT

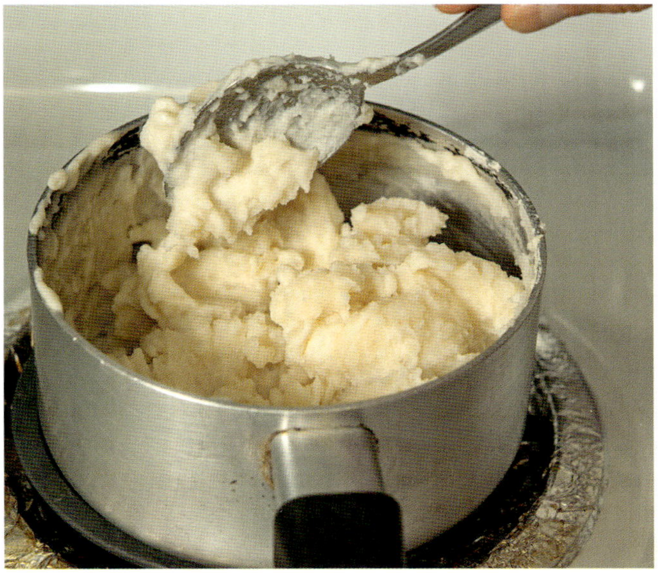

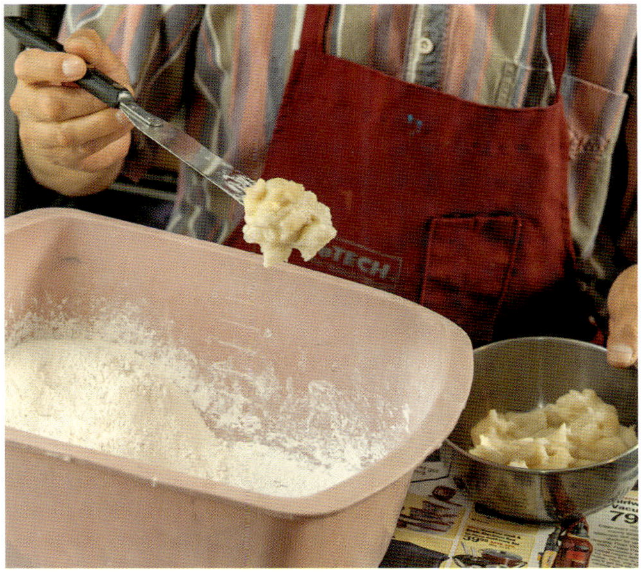

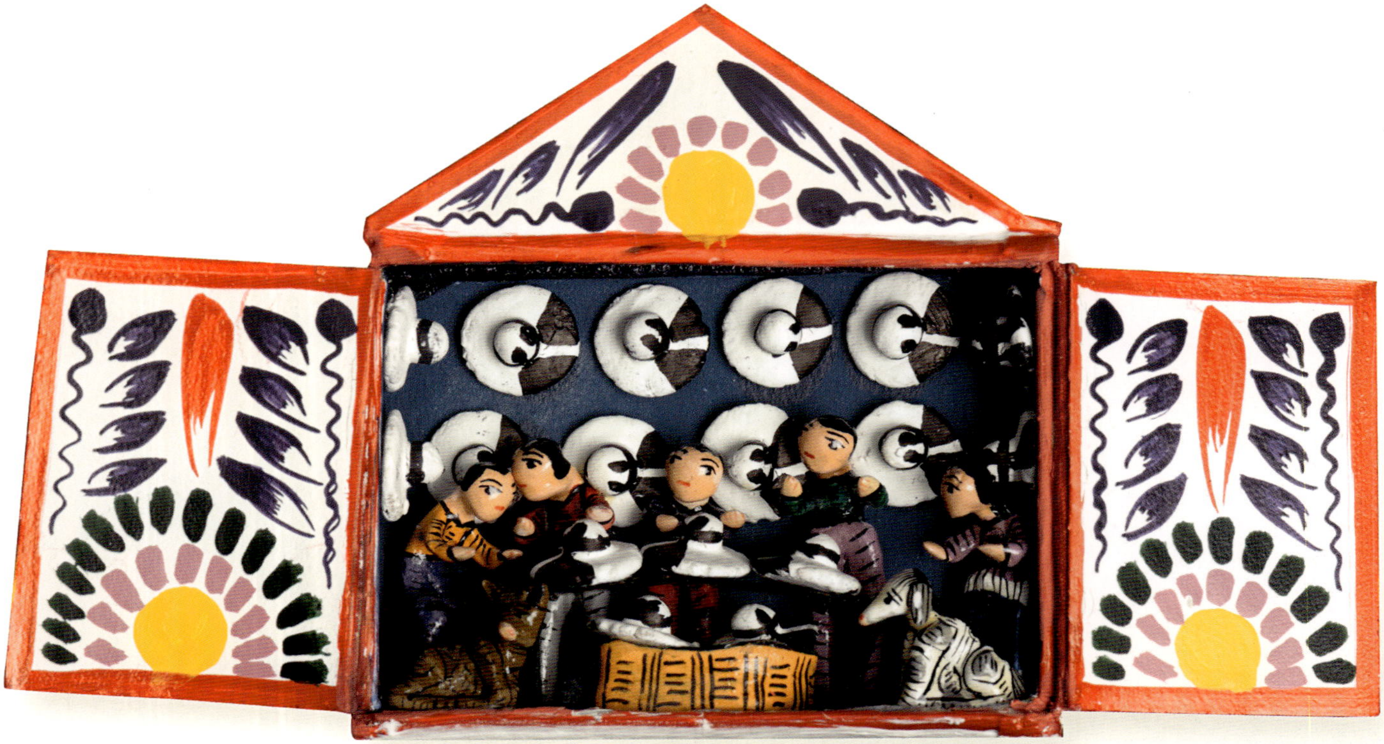

So, I repaired that retablo. I painted the figures with a natural color. And after a week, the lady came back to me and saw that I had finished it. She said she was pleased and said, "Thank you" to me. But she explained that she couldn't pay anything, because she had no money. In the market, we take no money. We give animals, produce, everything. She said they would bring me a small lamb. That was my pay. And I accepted it. It was okay.

When I was fourteen, I displayed my retablos for the first time in Huamanga, Peru. My father helped pick up my retablo, the whole mounting, and bring it to the city. It was before Easter, and in the city they had a very busy festival. And they displayed my retablo in a gallery in Huamanga. And there, I saw a very big retablo. I asked the man in the gallery who was the artist who made that retablo. His name was Joaquín López Antay, an old retablo maker in Huamanga. And I got to meet him. His clothing was very white. It was so hot, and he didn't speak Spanish, only Quechua.

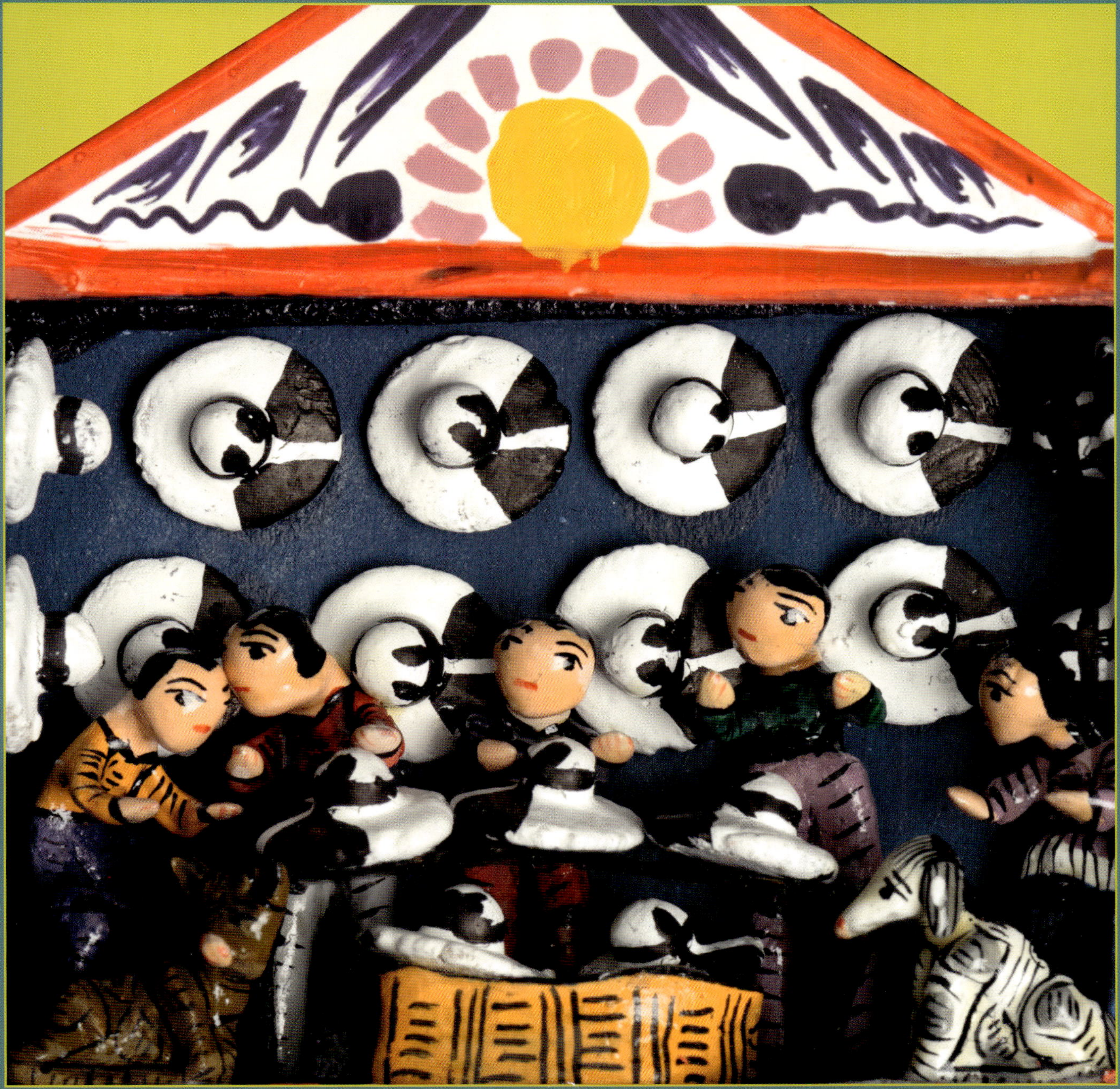

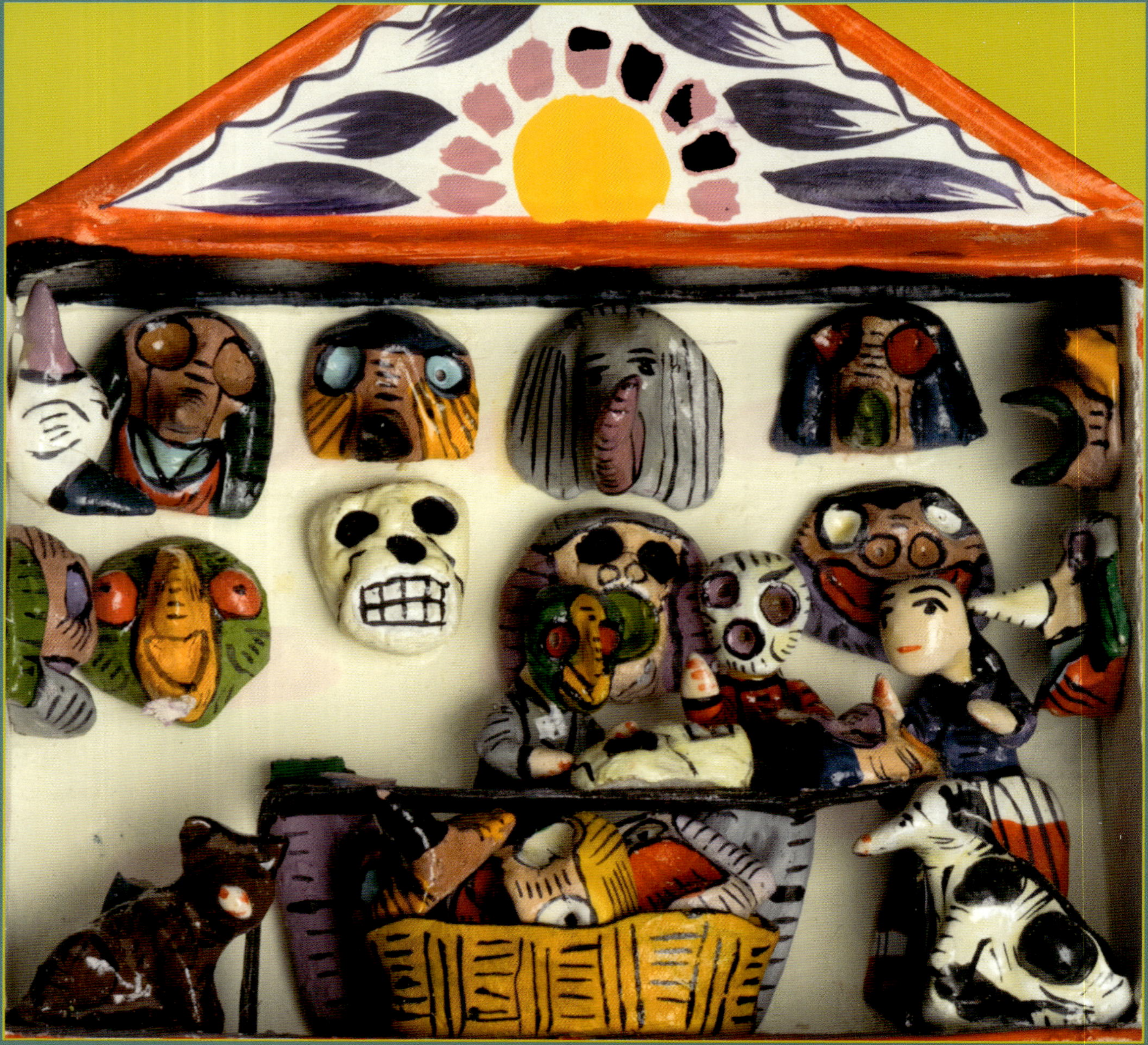

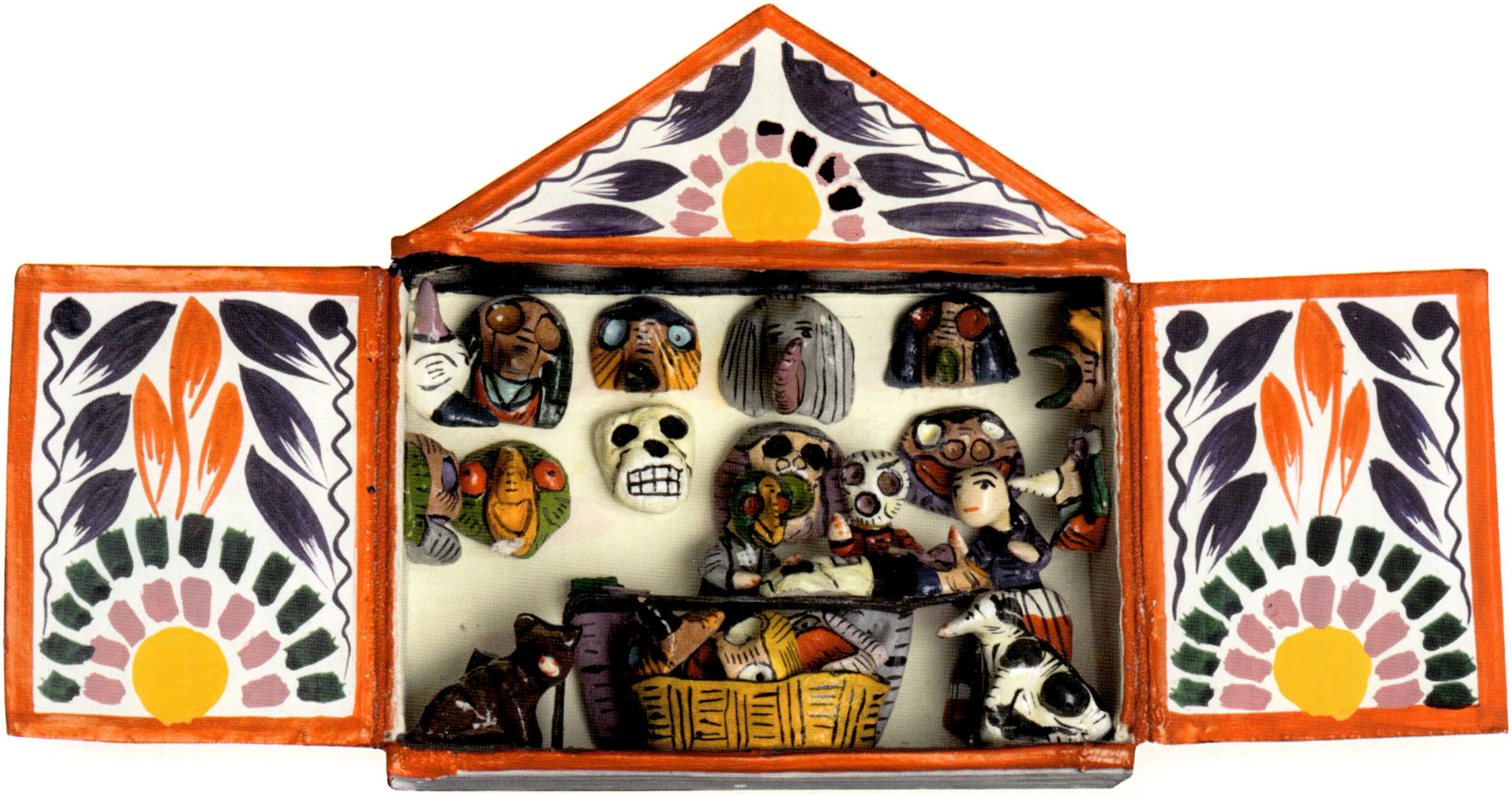

When I was sixteen, my parents took me to the city of Lima for my summer vacation from school. And they left me in Lima to stay with my aunt and uncle. When it was time go back to Ayacucho, I took a bus with my older brother Edilberto. And the bus had a very bad accident. It was in the night. The mountains are very steep, and the bus went over the edge and tumbled into the Mantaro River. There were forty-five passengers, and twelve people died. My brother and I survived. I could smell the blood, and they bandaged my head. I couldn't see or hear. It was very cold. The next morning, people came to help. There was no ambulance. They put me in a truck, and they took me to the hospital in Lima with the other injured people. My aunt and uncle saw it on the news and went to the hospital.

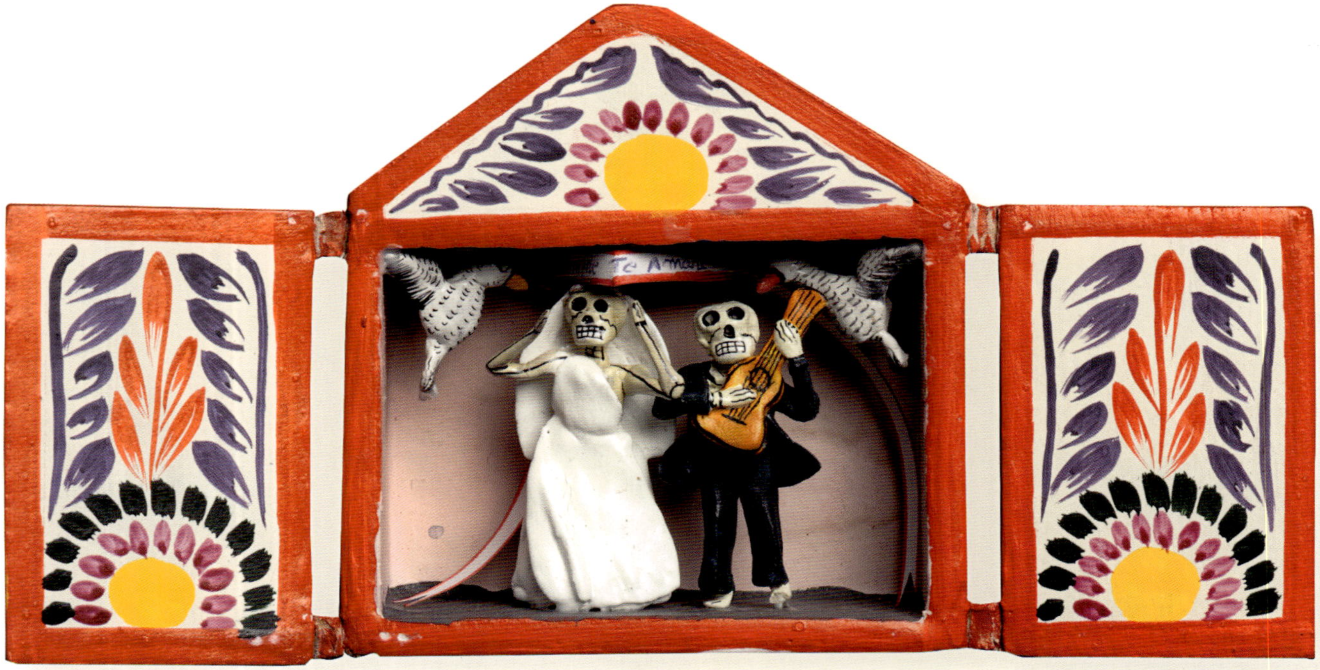

At the hospital, they took x-rays. I was in terrible pain, and they put me in a body cast because I had many broken ribs. My brother was also in the hospital, and his legs were broken. My aunt and uncle took us back to their home in Lima. After a month, my father came and took us back to the hospital in Huamanga for a checkup. And we went home to Rancha. I was in a body cast for a year.

After a very difficult year, I went back to the hospital, and they cut the cast off and did more x-rays. But the bones had not set right, and they pulled the ribs apart and put me into another cast for another six months.

But while I was in the body cast, I was also having problems with my ears. In Lima, the doctors had given me a treatment for my ears that I needed to use three times a day, but I got an infection. The left ear was worse, and the right was not nearly as bad. But the infection went on for years, and I lost my hearing.

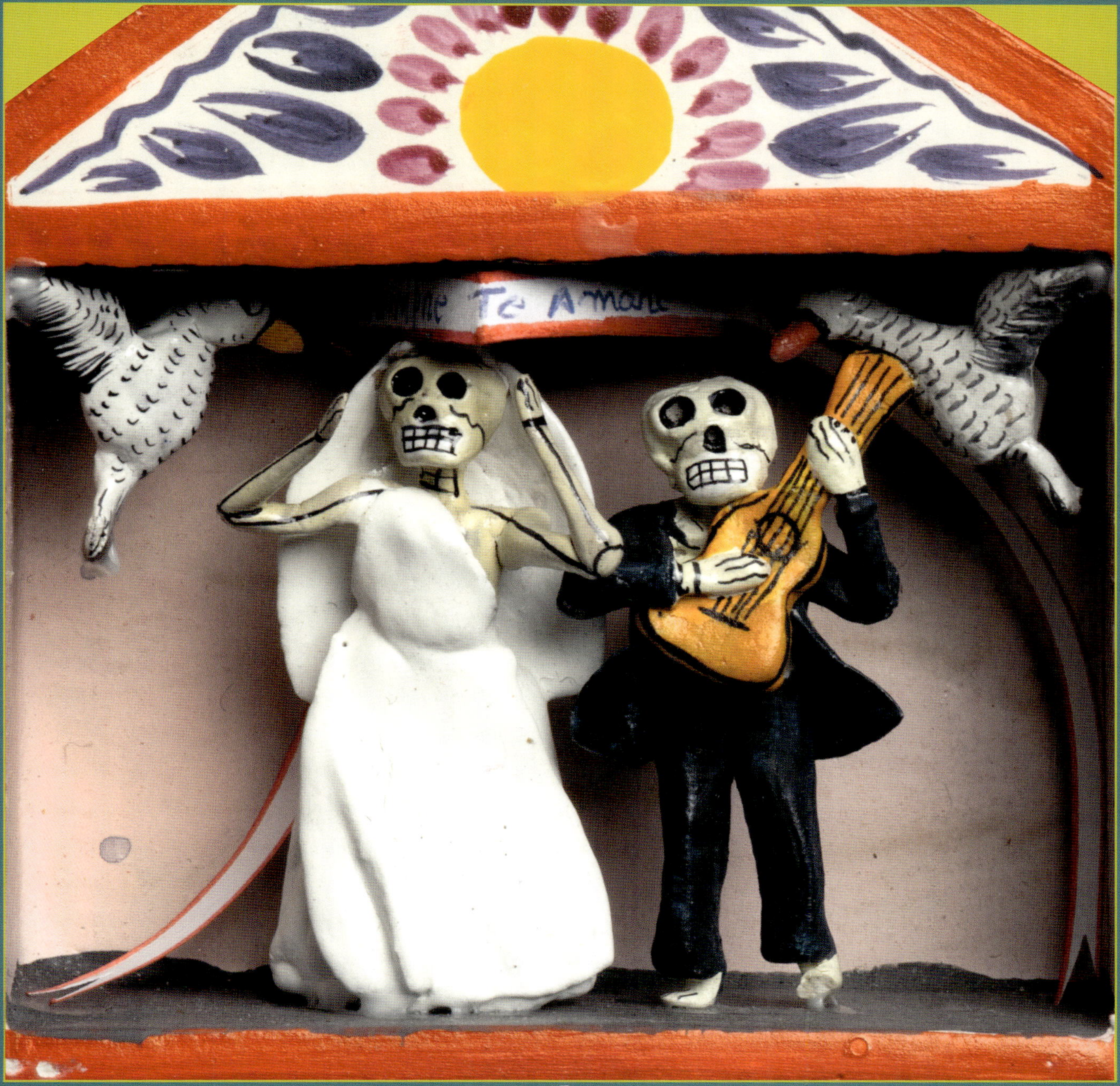

After I got out of the body cast, I went to art school during the day and finished my high school classes at night. Up until that time, I spoke only Quechua, but I took high school classes and began to learn to speak Spanish.

My brother Edilberto played piano for the local Catholic church, and the friar took me into a separate room that had all these books in Spanish. And I taught myself to read Spanish, with help from the friar.

A few years later, after my accident, I went back to Huamanga and showed Joaquín López Antay my retablo, and he saw that mine was molded by hand and that it was different, better. So, he told me he was going to the city of Lima. I accompanied him, and I received a big award, recognition.

In the mountains, we had many traditions, customs, and dances. We celebrated independence with a bullfight. And in my village, we had traditional dance. Every year, we had Christmas dances. And we decorated festive clothing. The competition was one man with another man. Other dances had the ladies with other ladies. The competition went on for three days. In the finale, the judges decided who won.

When I traveled in the mountains, I heard very nice singing, songs in Quechua. And I learned them, before I lost my hearing. So, I sing in Quechua, and some songs I also mix with Spanish. Also, I learned dances. Everything I learned about singing and dancing I have depicted in my retablos.

Whenever I had school vacation, I went back to the mountains to little villages and studied the traditions and traditional arts. That went on for seven years. I wanted to learn and be aware of the music, dance, and folk arts of the different cultures and the people who lived there.

I studied art in Huamanga and started teaching in Quechua different folk arts and music and dance in a school that I started. And when I brought my retablos to Lima, I was invited to become a teacher of art in a high school.

In 1994, I came to the United States with a Peruvian folk arts group. We were invited to Utah, to a town called Bountiful north of Salt Lake City. We performed our dances and the traditional music of Peru on our handmade instruments. I brought everything I owned with me: my retablos, wood carvings and paintings, and a big cross with the crucifixion that I had made with different figures and symbols. I hoped that there would be a way for me to stay in the United States.

I had a temporary visa, but I wanted to extend it. As part of the process of extending the visa, I had to be checked by a doctor because they were aware I had a hearing problem. After asking around, I met a doctor through a friend I had made named Kirk Henrichsen, who became my patron. With Kirk's help, the first doctor I found looked at my ears, and he said he couldn't do anything about my hearing loss.

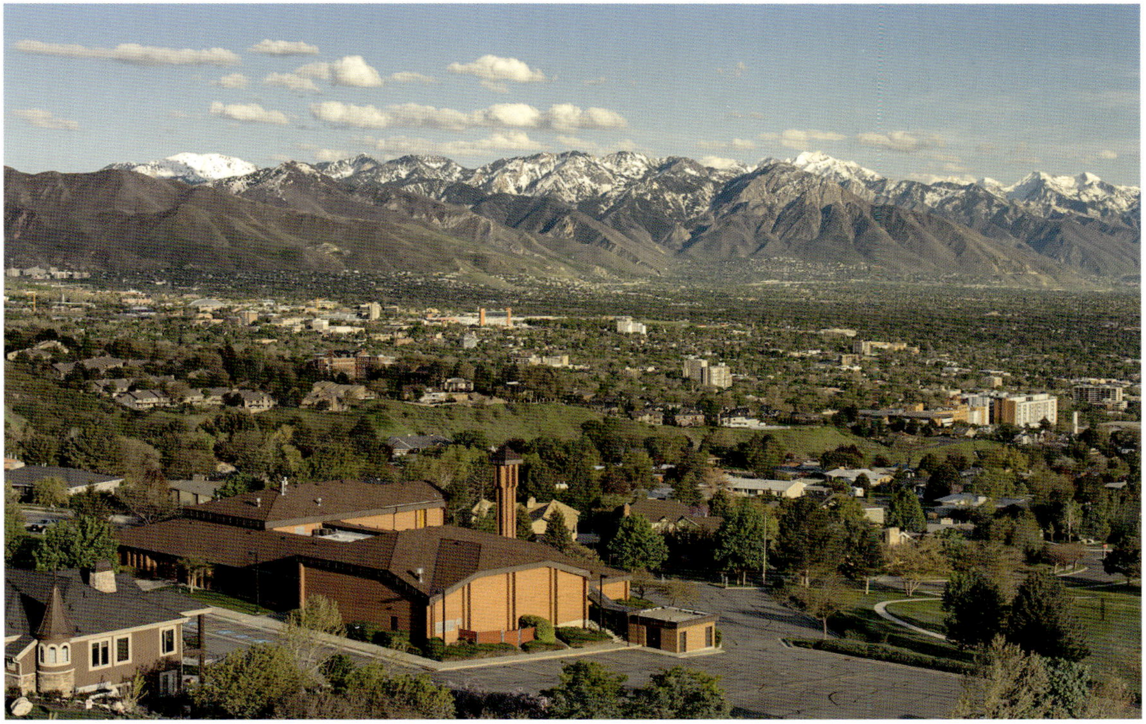

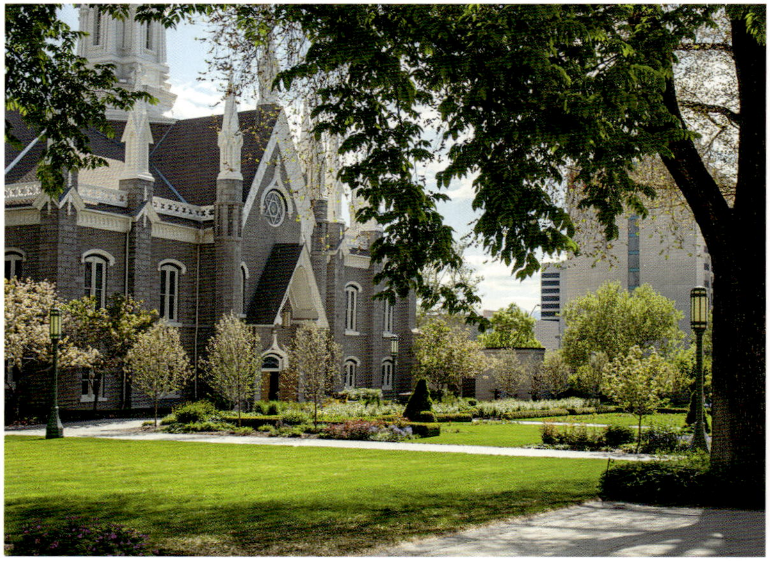

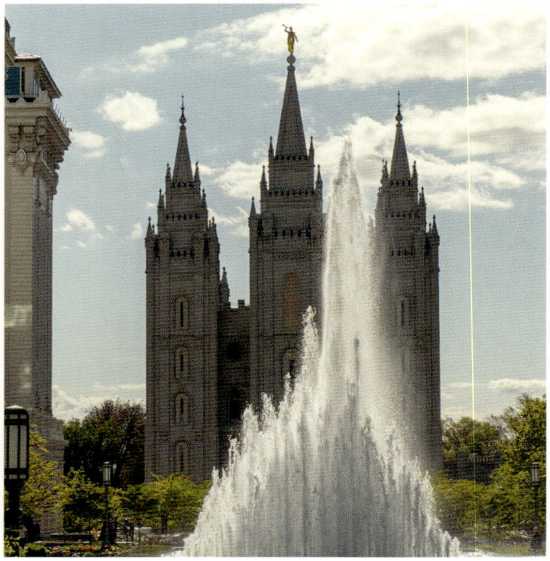

By the beginning of 1995, I had started to learn about the Church of Jesus Christ of Latter-day Saints. They had a church near where I was living in Murray, Utah. I met a man who was American and was married to a Peruvian woman, and they invited me to go to church with them. The service was in Spanish. I read the Book of Mormon and was baptized into the church.

Because I had received attention in Utah from the art I had brought, I was on television and in the newspaper. People in the Mormon Church were aware of who I was. They introduced me to the bishop, who offered to help with my hearing problems.

Kirk Henrichsen got a recommendation for me to go to a different specialist. After the examination, he urged me to go see a top hearing surgeon at the University of Utah. His name was Dr. Clough Shelton, a professor and chief of the hearing department. And when he looked in my ears, he saw the complete destruction of the membranes of my inner ear, with high levels of infection. He said I needed surgery, but I didn't have the money for the operation. So, the surgeon told me that he could go to the LDS Hospital, operated by the Mormon Church, and he would do the surgery through charity. And I had an operation that

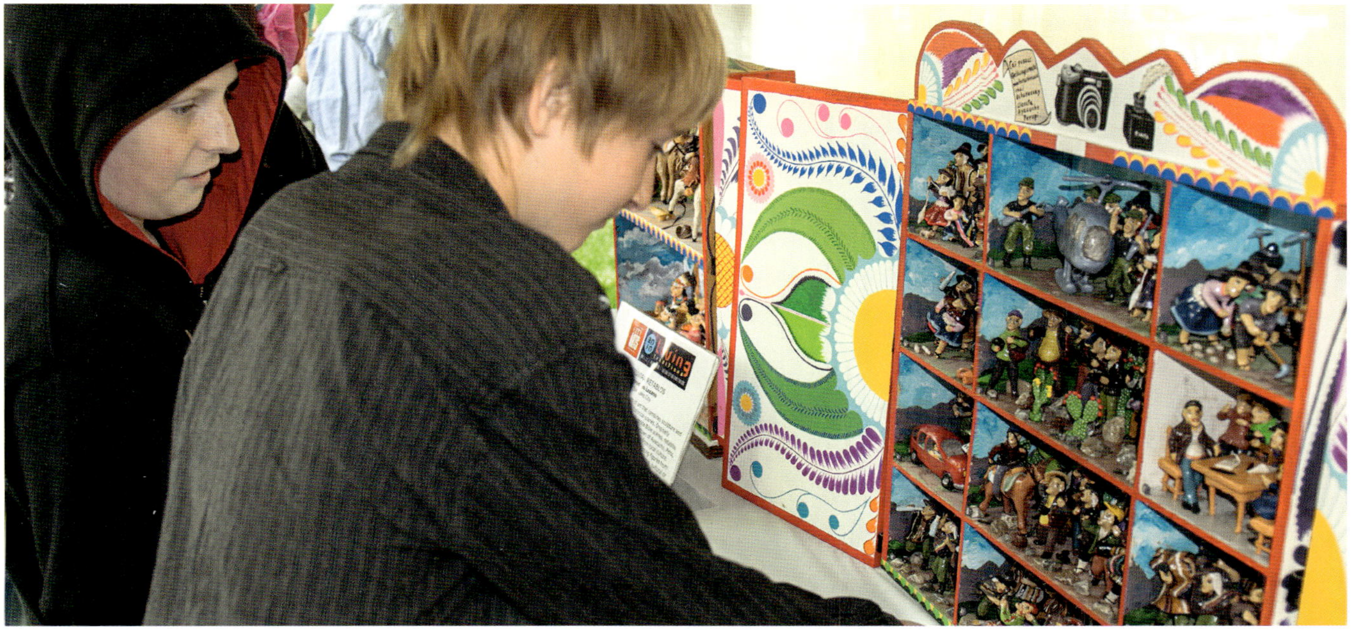

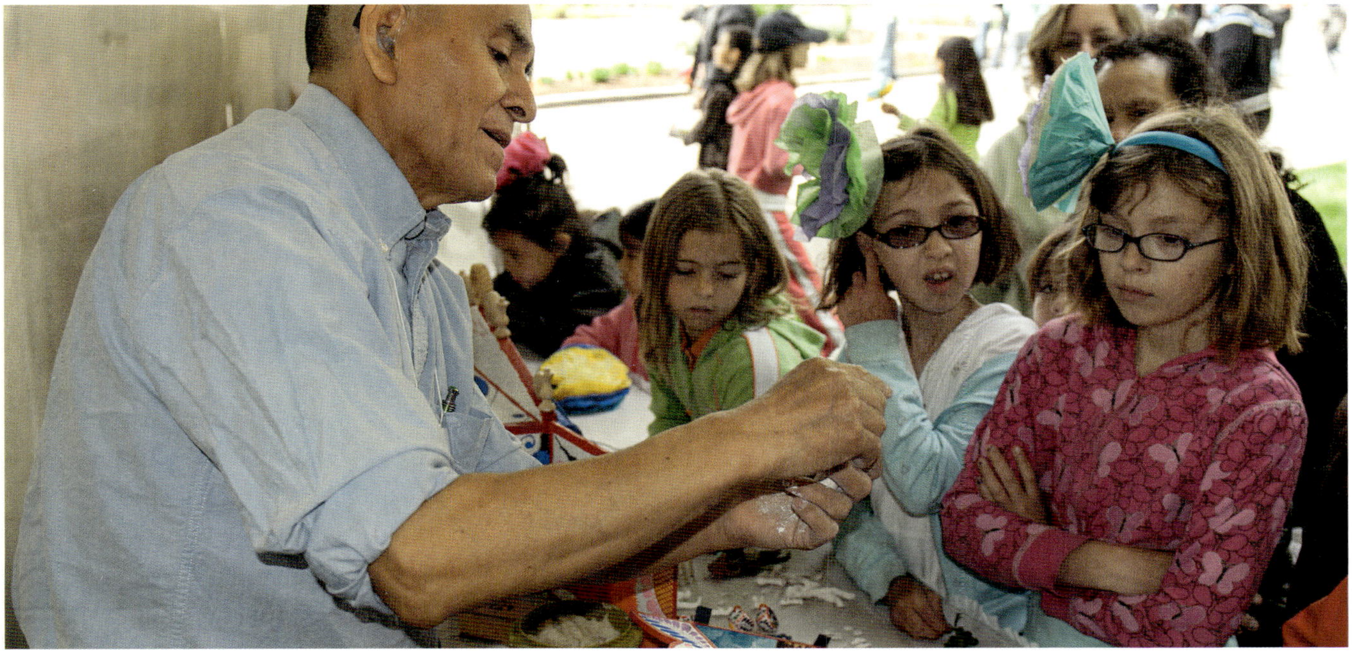

replaced my eardrum. And after my surgery, a woman named Mary Dunn offered to take me to her apartment in Midvale, Utah, for me to recuperate. After some time in her care, the doctors took the bandages off my left ear. For the first time, I heard the very beautiful voice of Mary, and also the beautiful singing of birds outside the window. Mary and I were so happy that we gave great thanks, praying to God. I later got a hearing aid to be able to hear better. And to this day, I have hearing aids for both ears.

I eventually got my visa extended. And as I got more recognition for my art, they approved me, saying I was a benefit to my new country. With Kirk's help, I am now a citizen of the United States. Today, I have my new life here. I give thanks for that, for more life. I keep working.

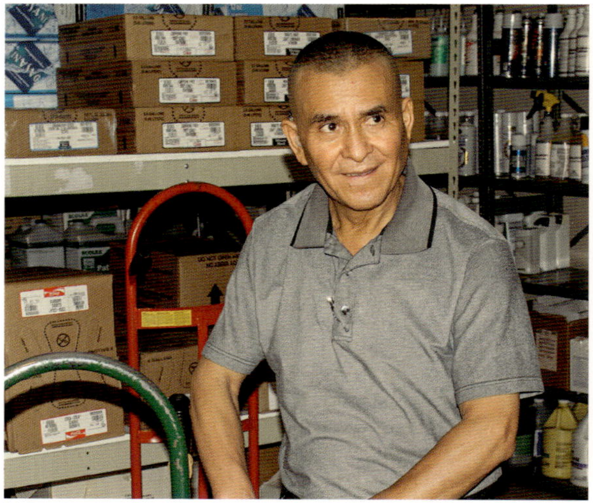

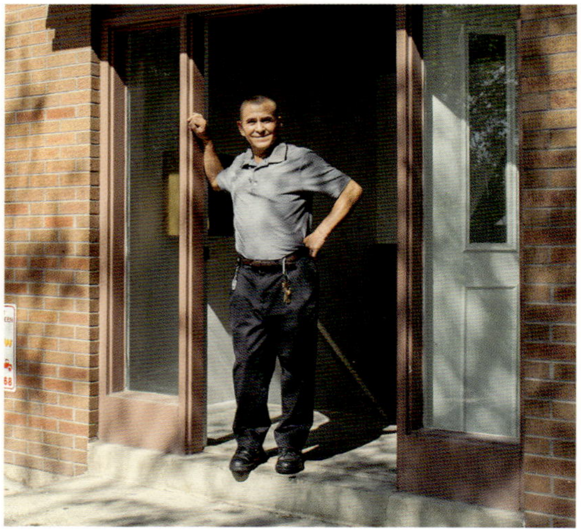

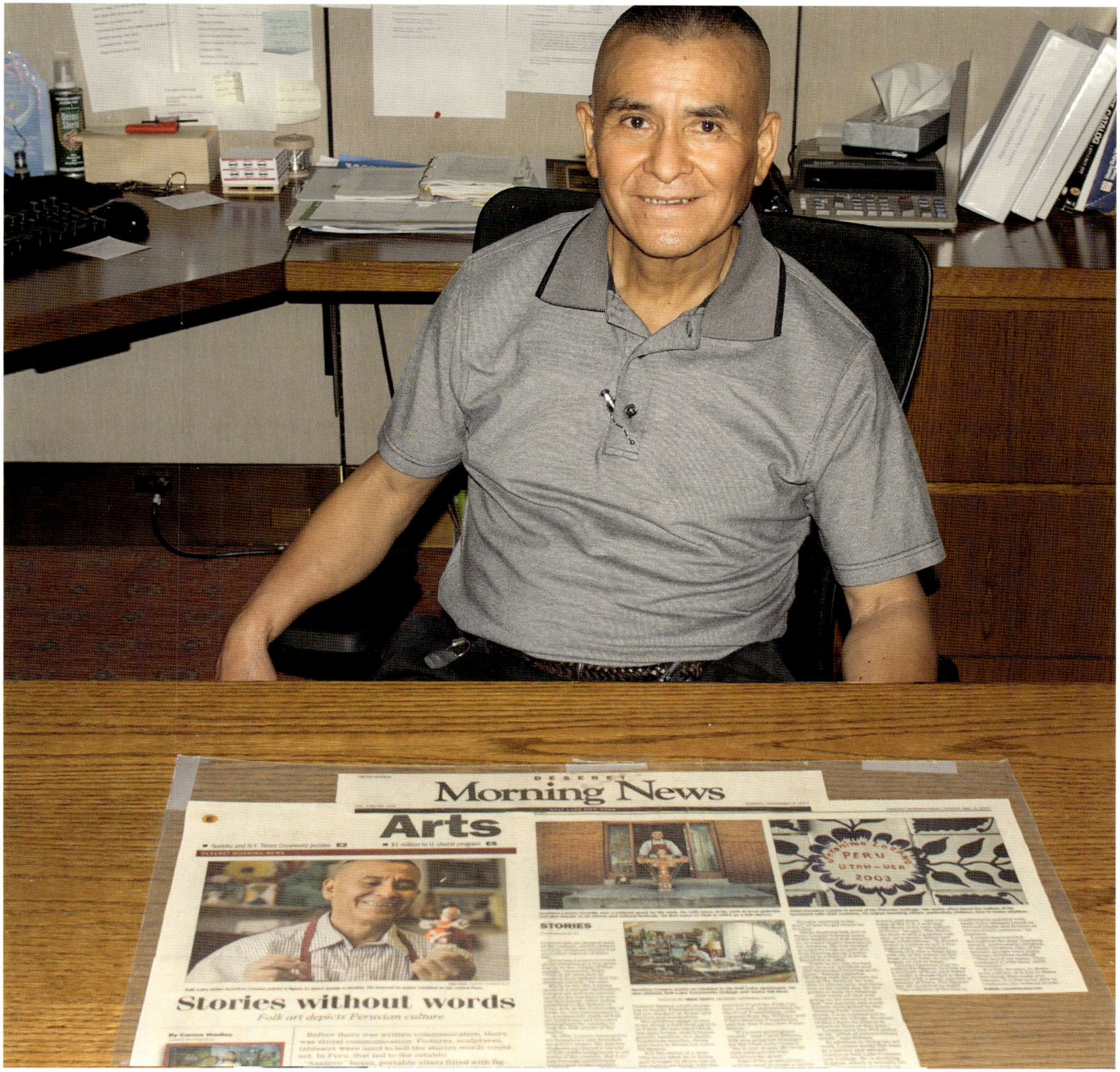
DESERET
Morning News
Arts
Stories without words
Folk art depicts Peruvian culture
STORIES
PERU
UTAH - USA
2003

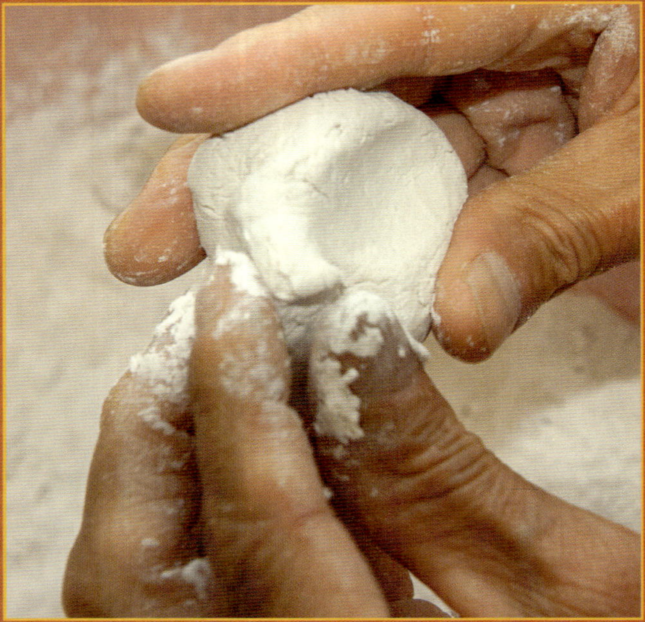

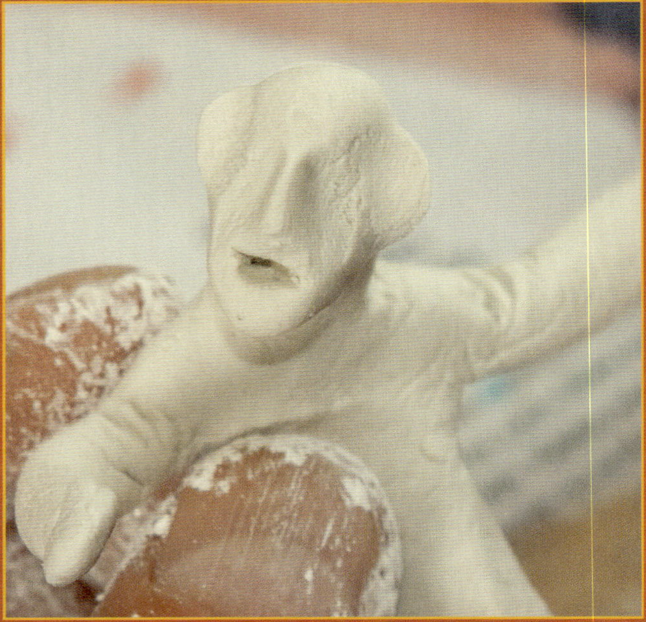

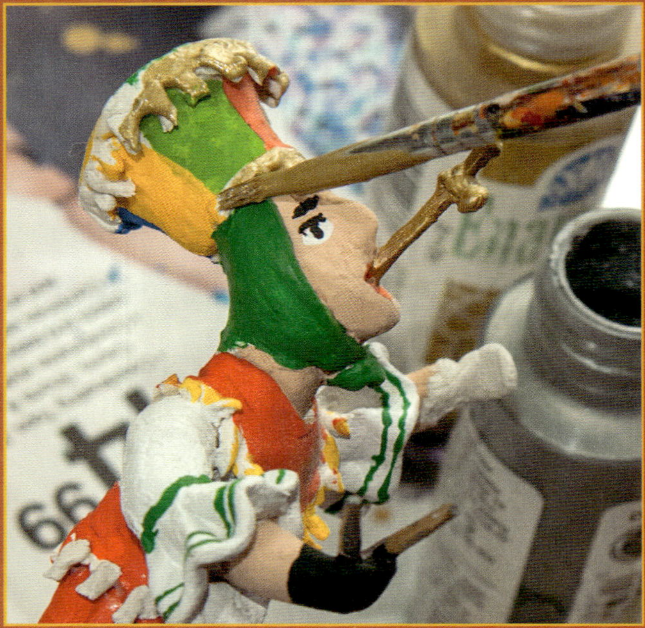

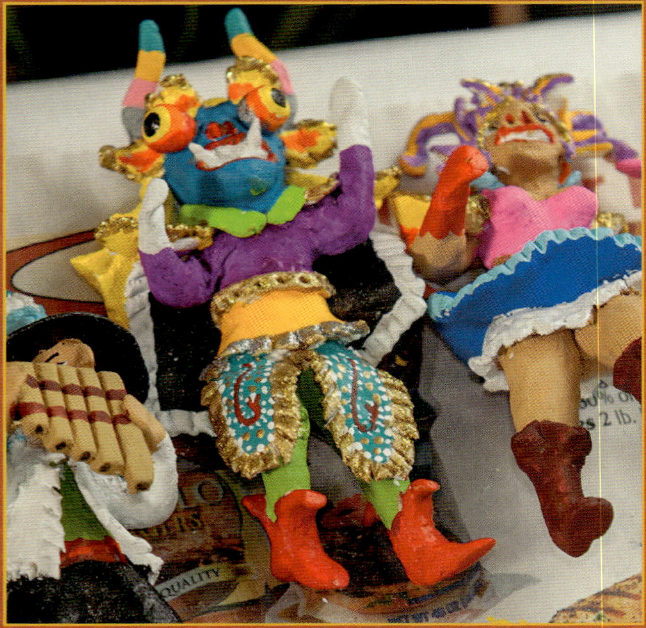

My Process

Retablos I make can take three days or one week, because it is not very easy. It's necessary to wait for the figures to dry, and I must dry the clothing that I want for the people to wear. Then I paint the figures and the clothing and decorate the box for the figures I place inside. A large retablo might take two or three months, because there are many figures in the different boxes, and the painting in the boxes is more difficult.

For many years, I made retablos depicting saints—different saints for people in different places. I began to search for new ideas and decided to make retablos to show different customs, and even political events and social dramas.

The figures in a traditional San Marcos box—the saint's boxes, as they were called—were made from press-molded plaster molds. They would press a material into the molds. One of the things that I was recognized for doing was innovating handcrafted modeled figures, rather than molded figures. The material that I began using was taking the traditional baked potato of Peru and creating a paste out of the potato. I'm not sure if they boiled the potato down to flour or just took the mashed-up potato and mixed it, but I mixed it with naturally occurring plaster (*jaso*) that I would dig in the mountains, and the combination of the two created a very hard modeling paste that dried hard because of the plaster.

Today, here in the United States, what I mix up is wheat paste, because wheat flour is easier to find than potato flour, and then I add plaster of paris to that, so that the wheat paste then hardens as the plaster of paris sets up. So, after mixing the two ingredients together, I have about half an hour to model the figure, before it starts to become stiff and is no longer flexible.

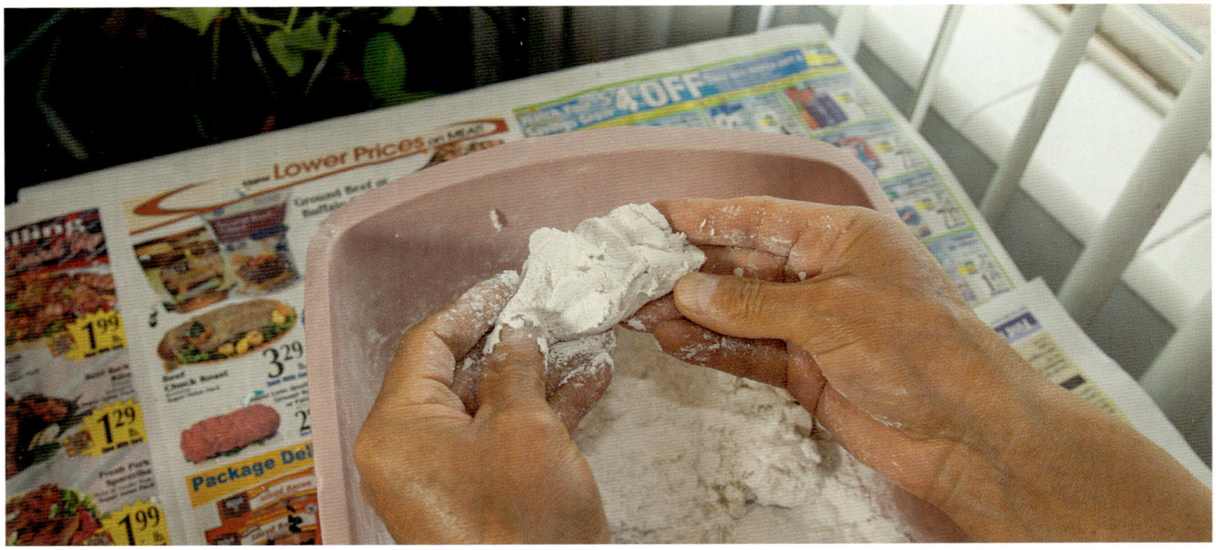
Lower Prices

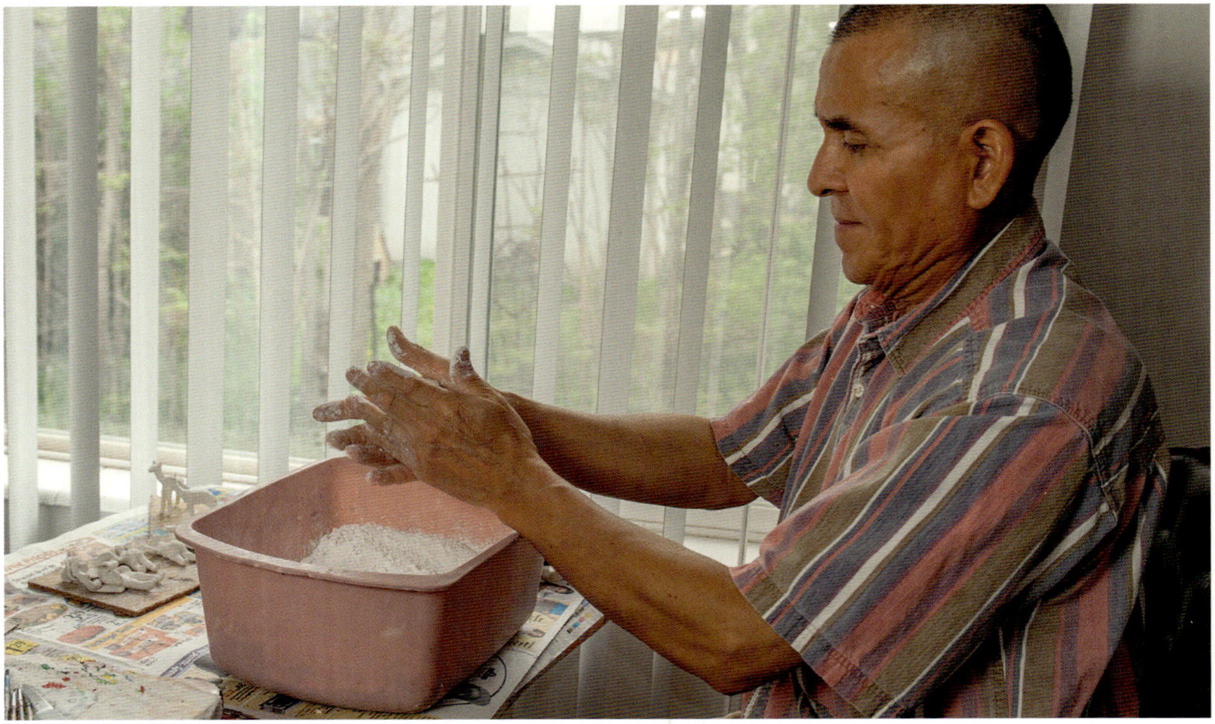

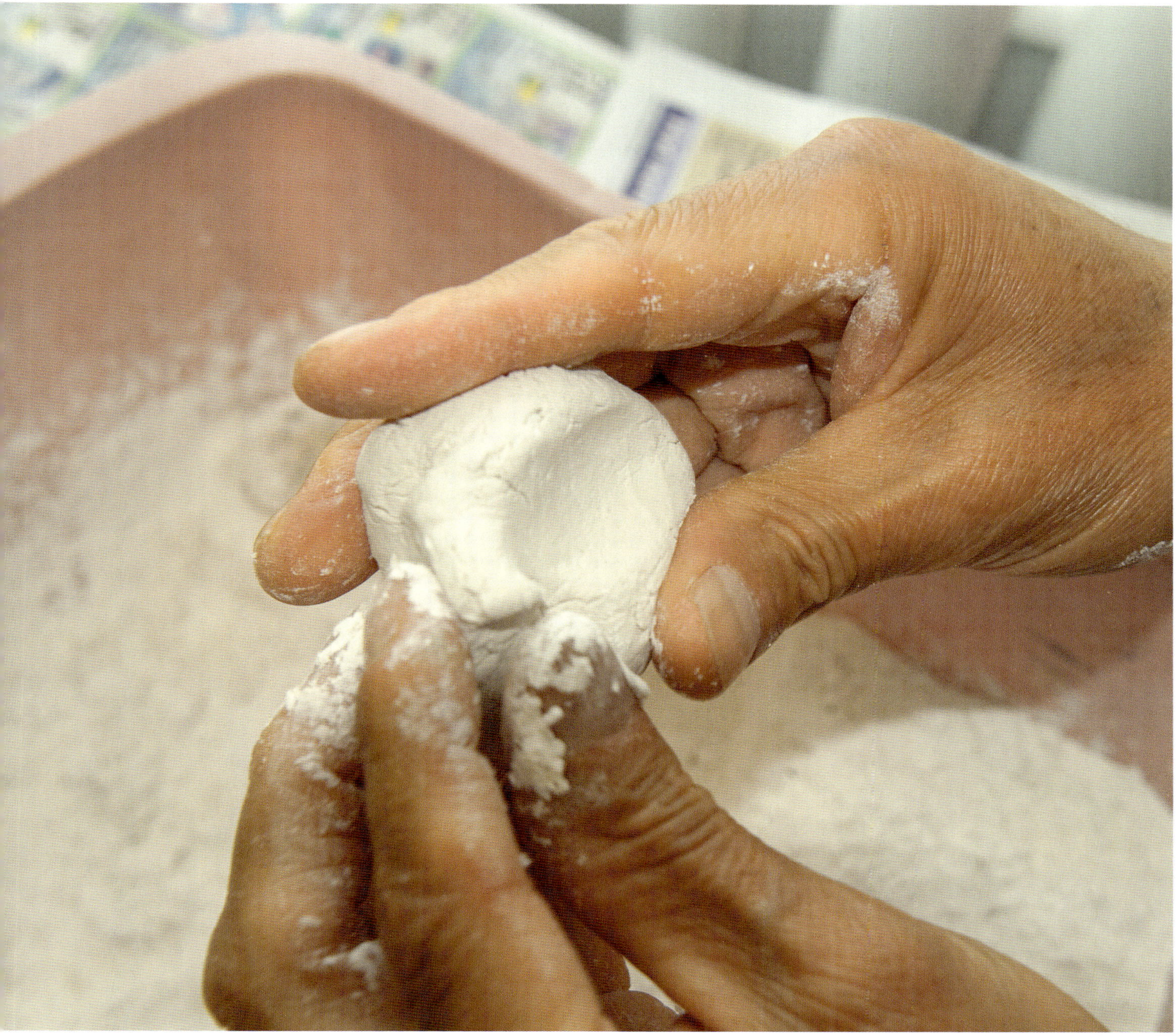

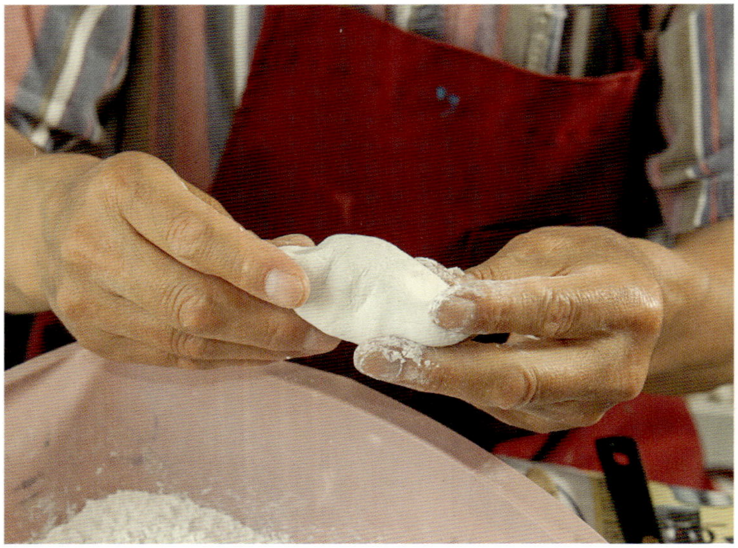

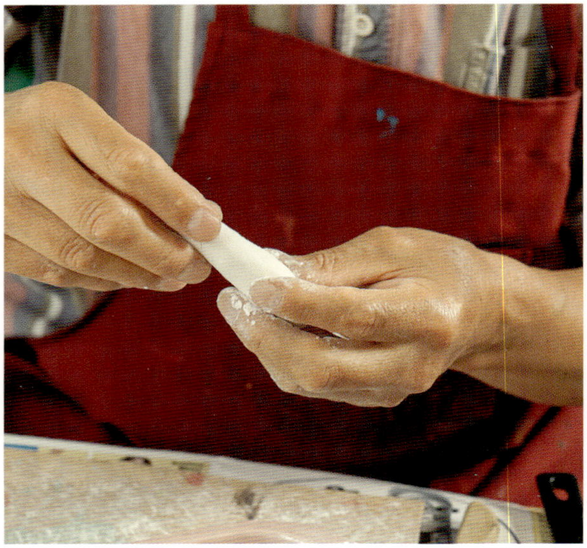

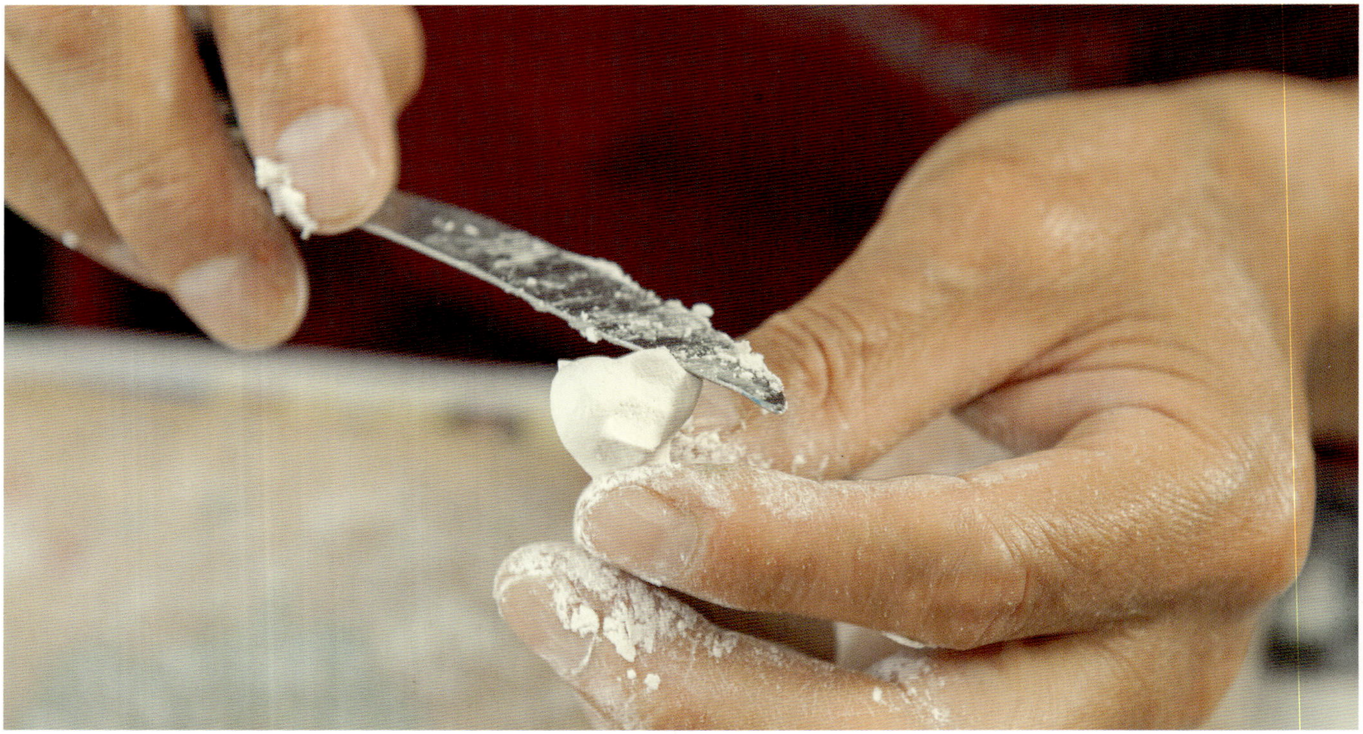

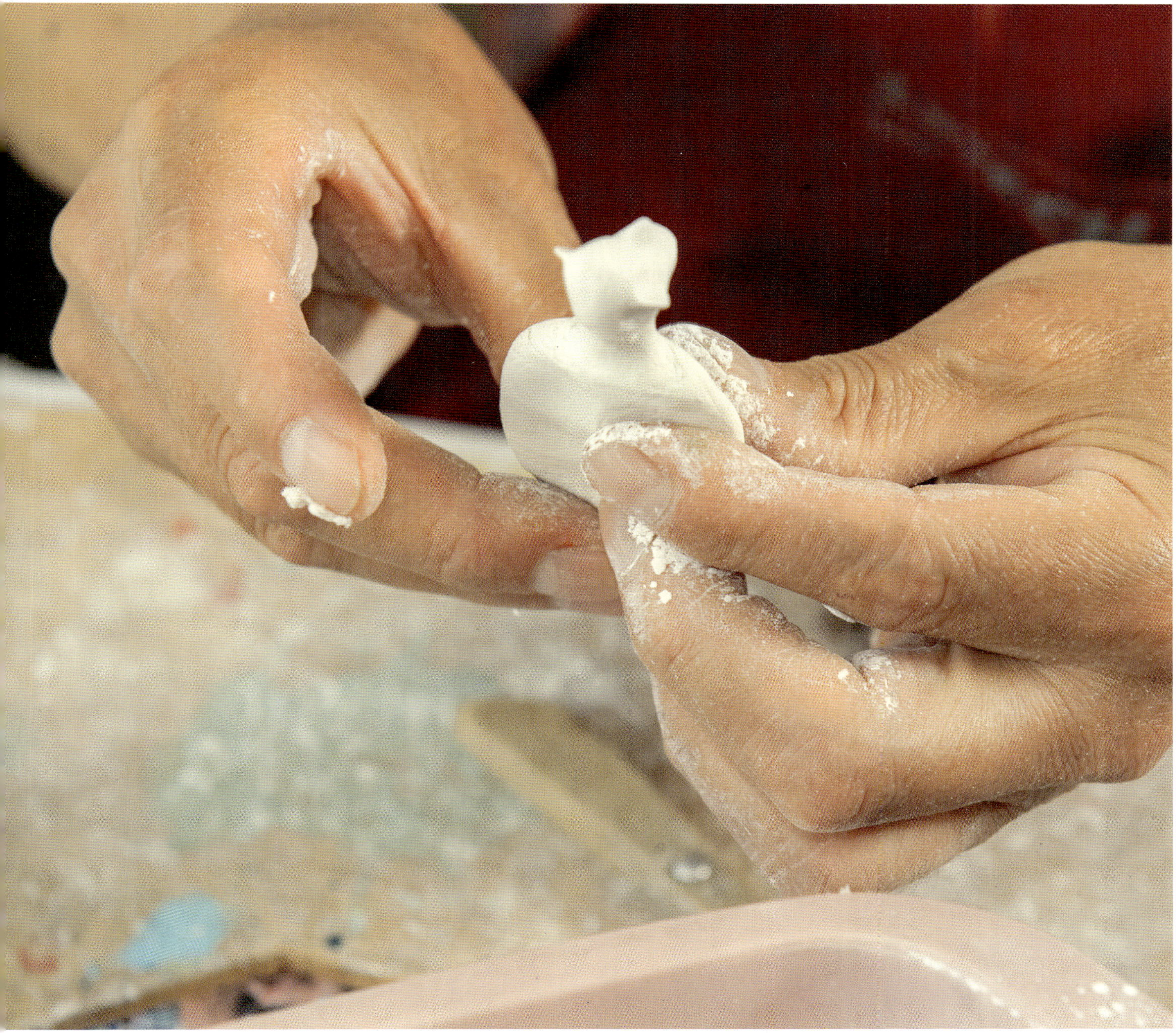

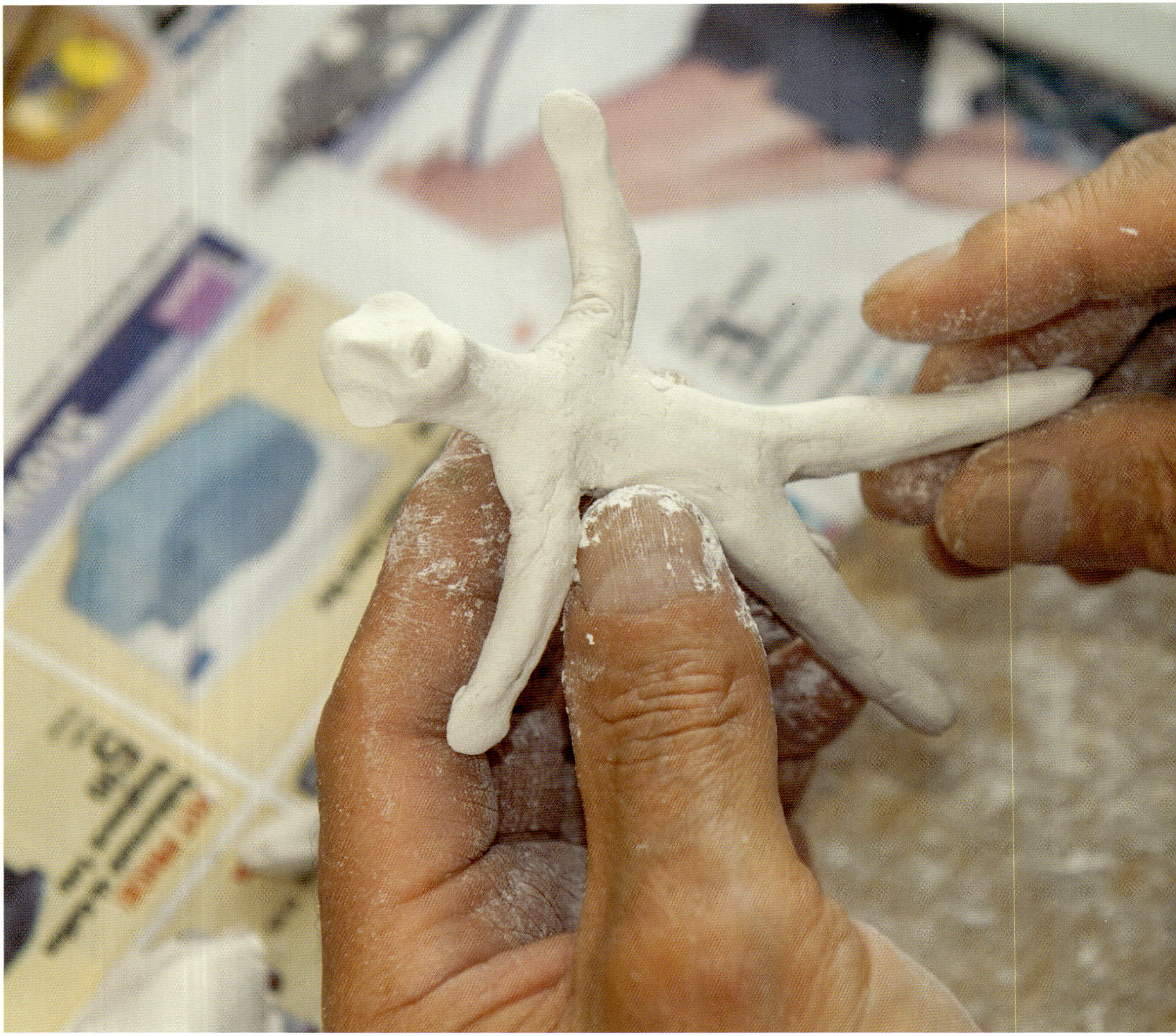

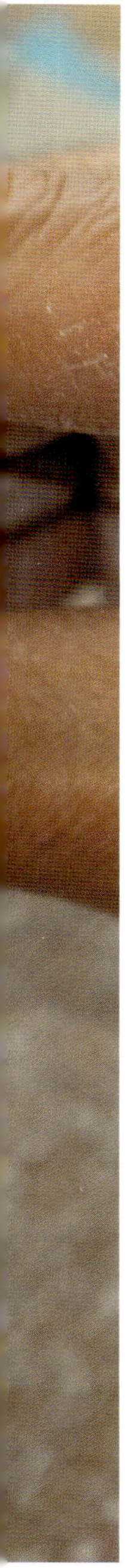

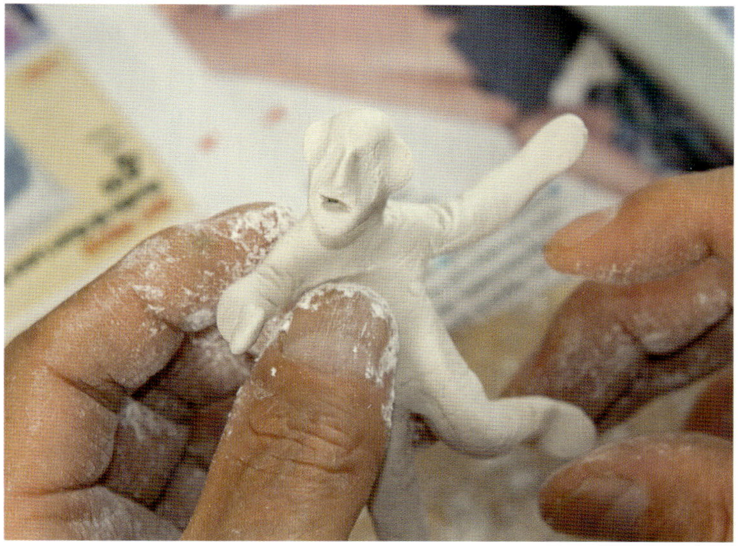

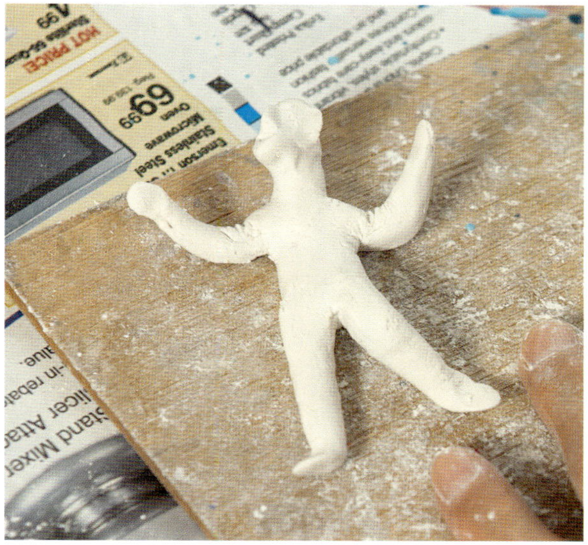

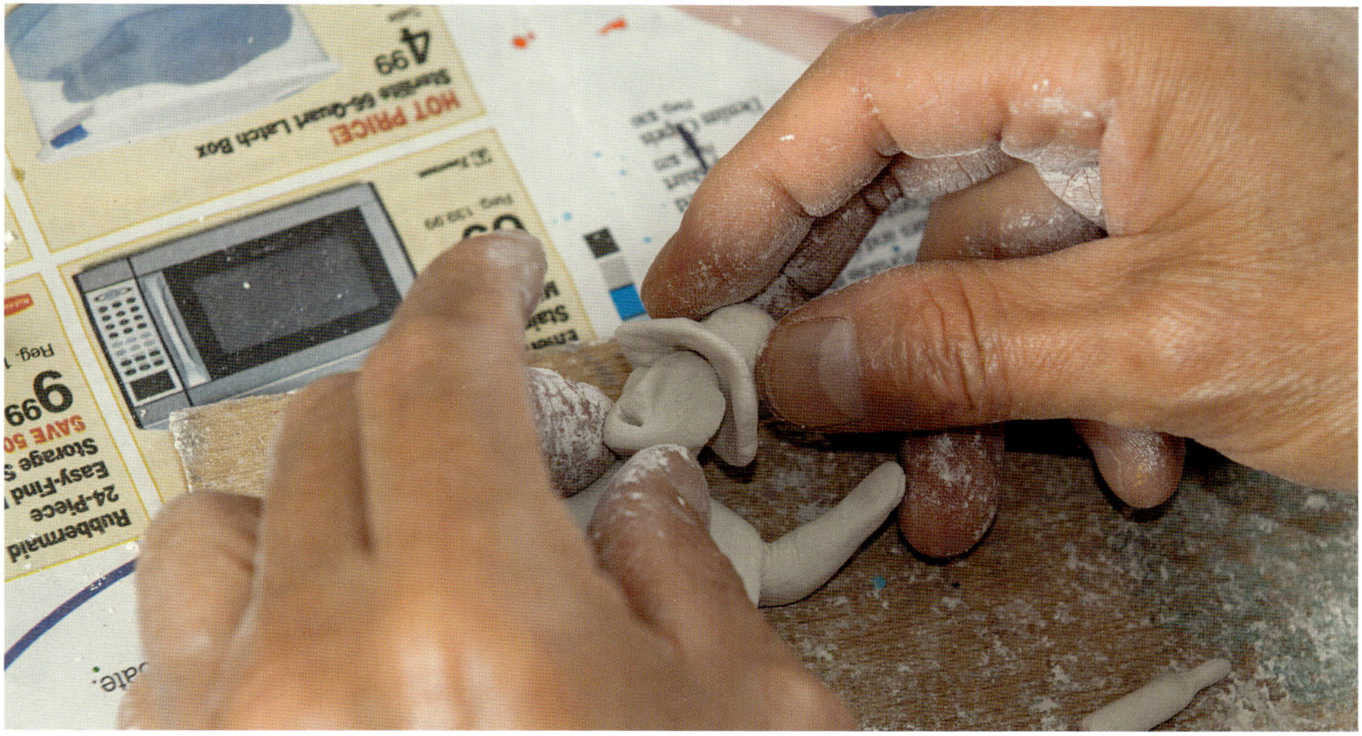

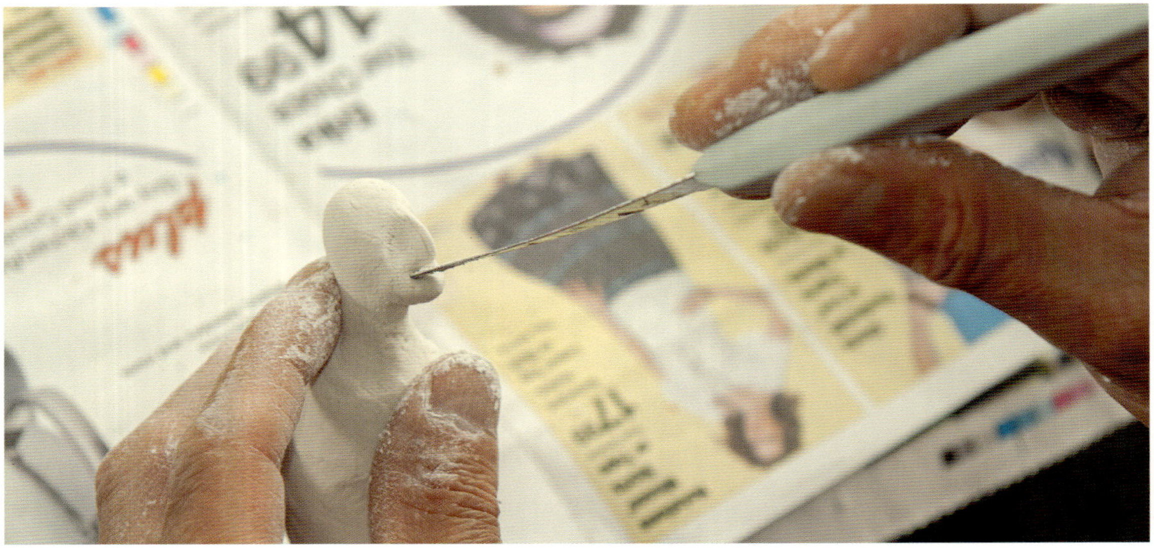

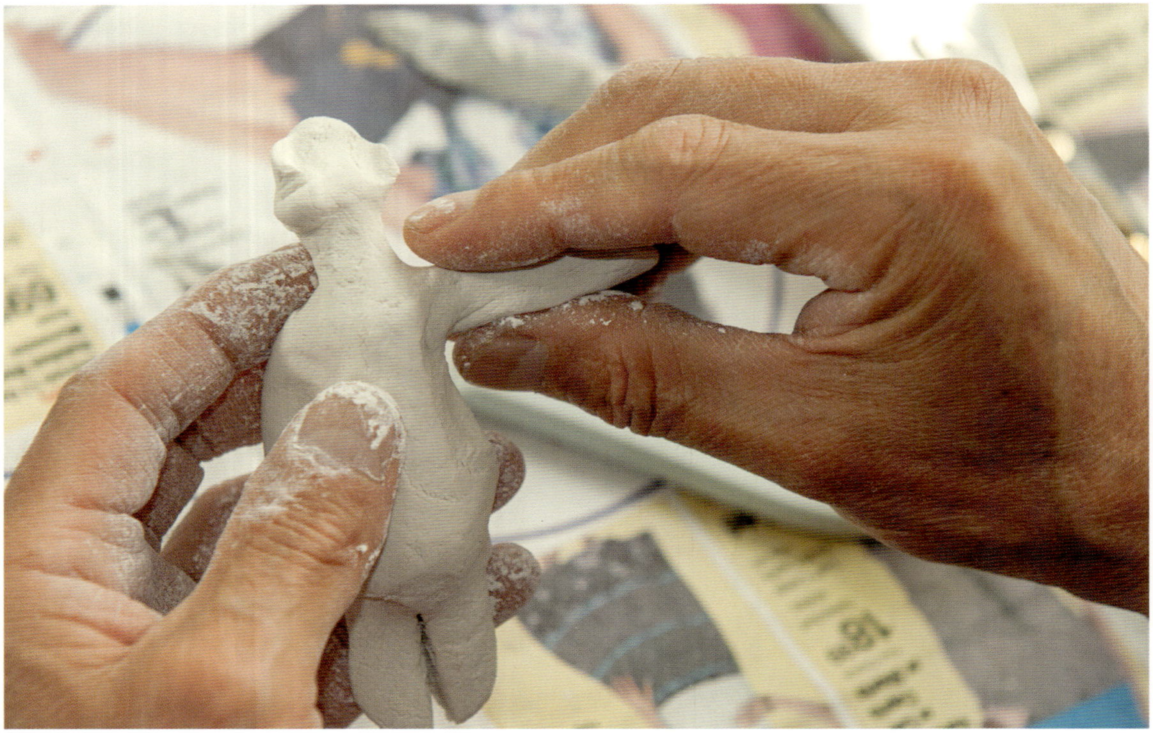

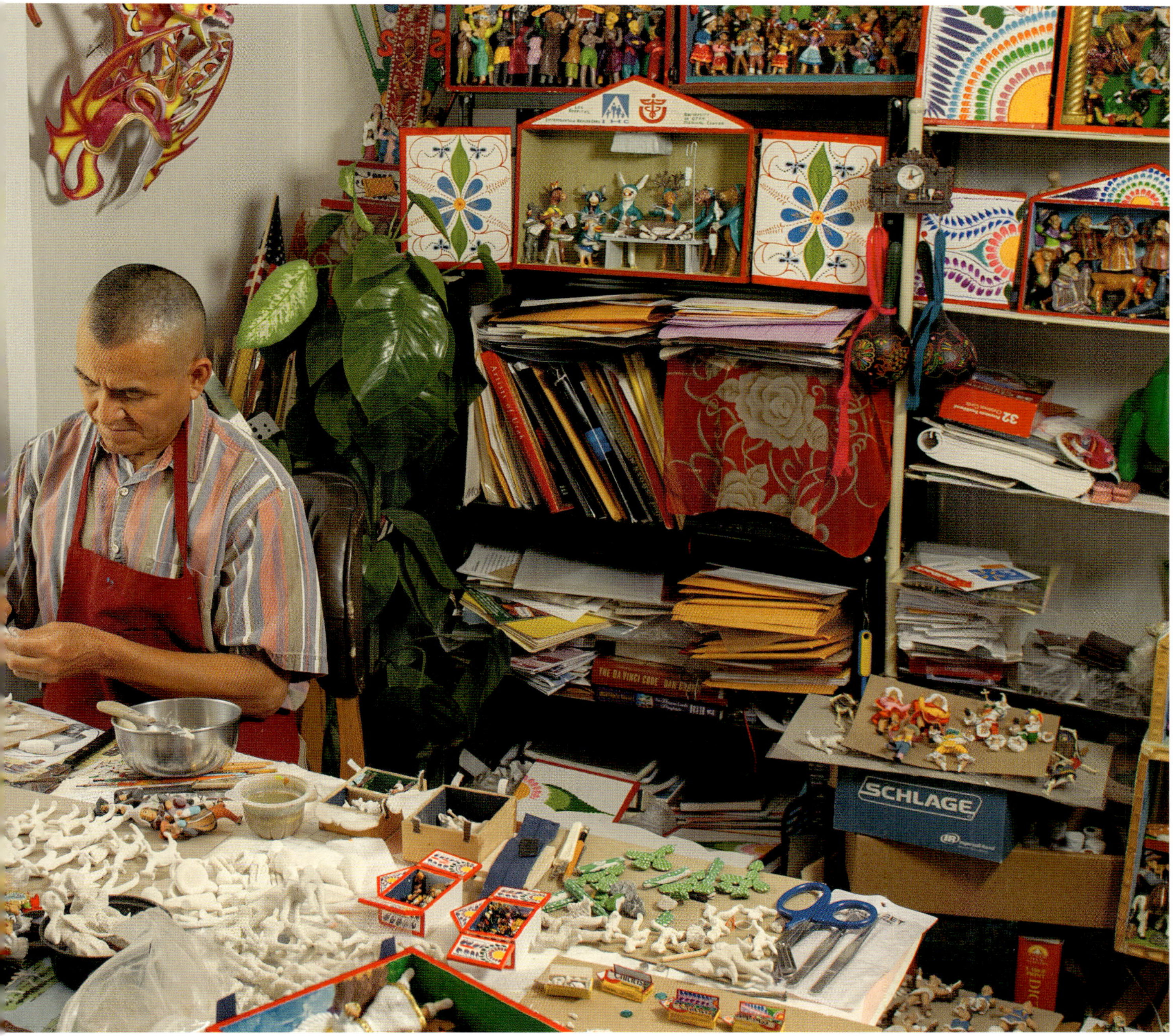
SCHLAGE

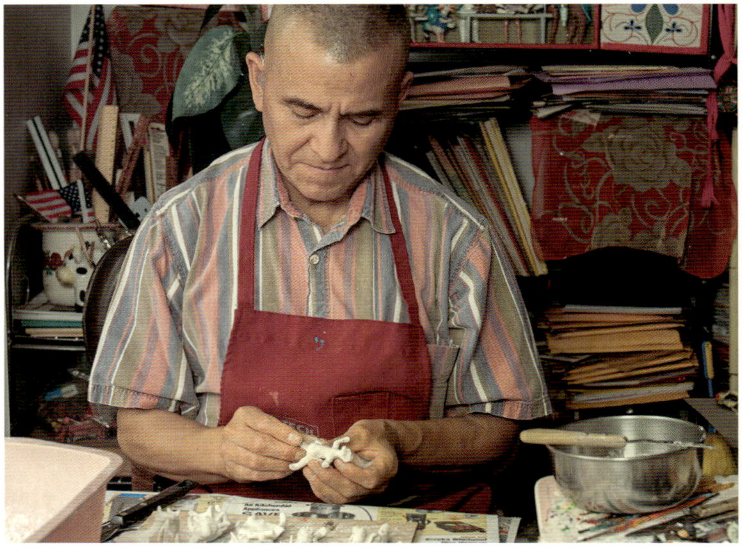

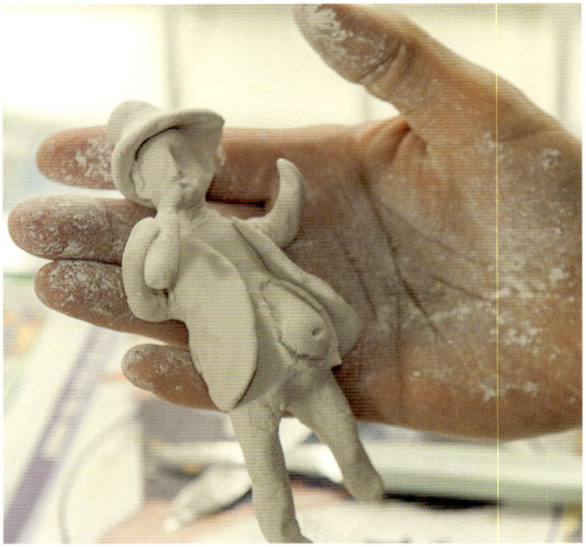

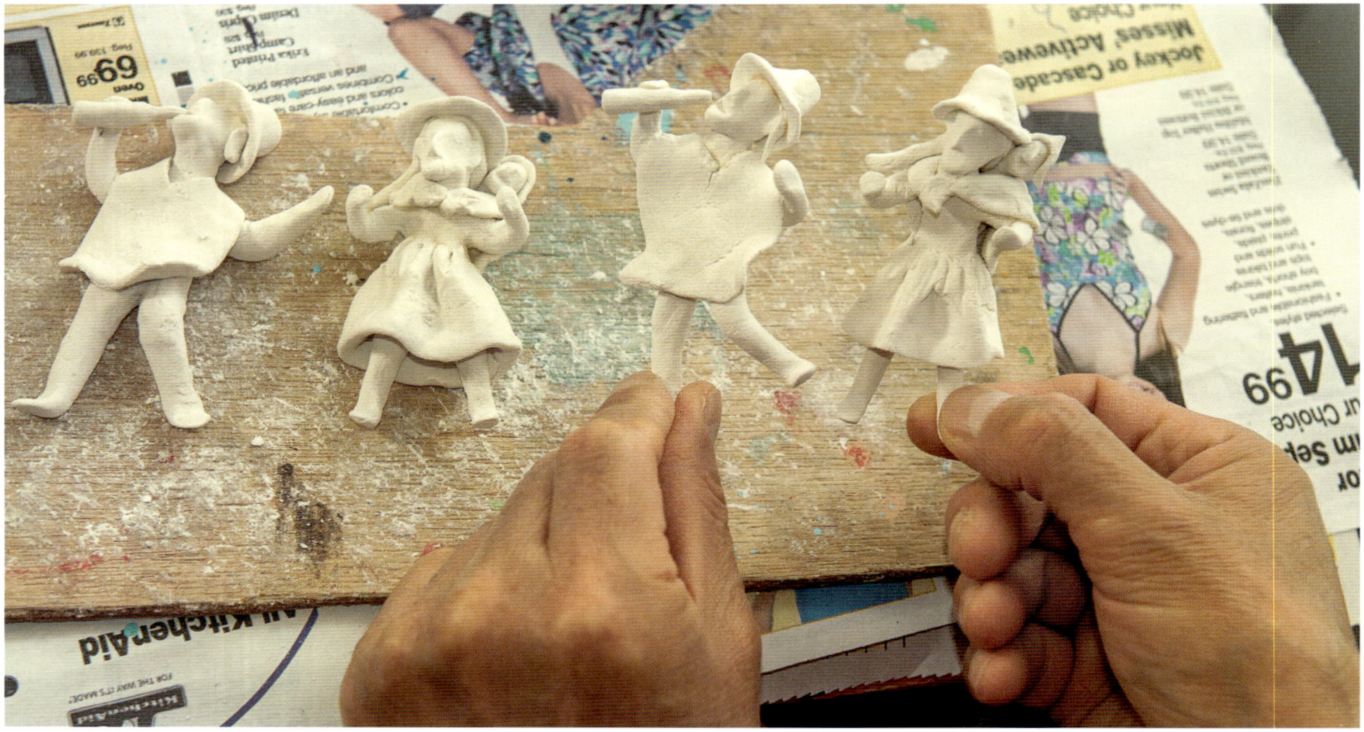

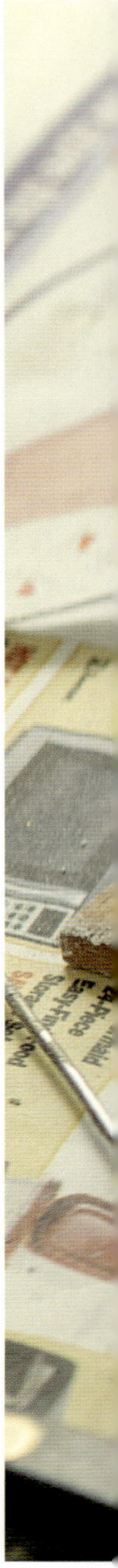

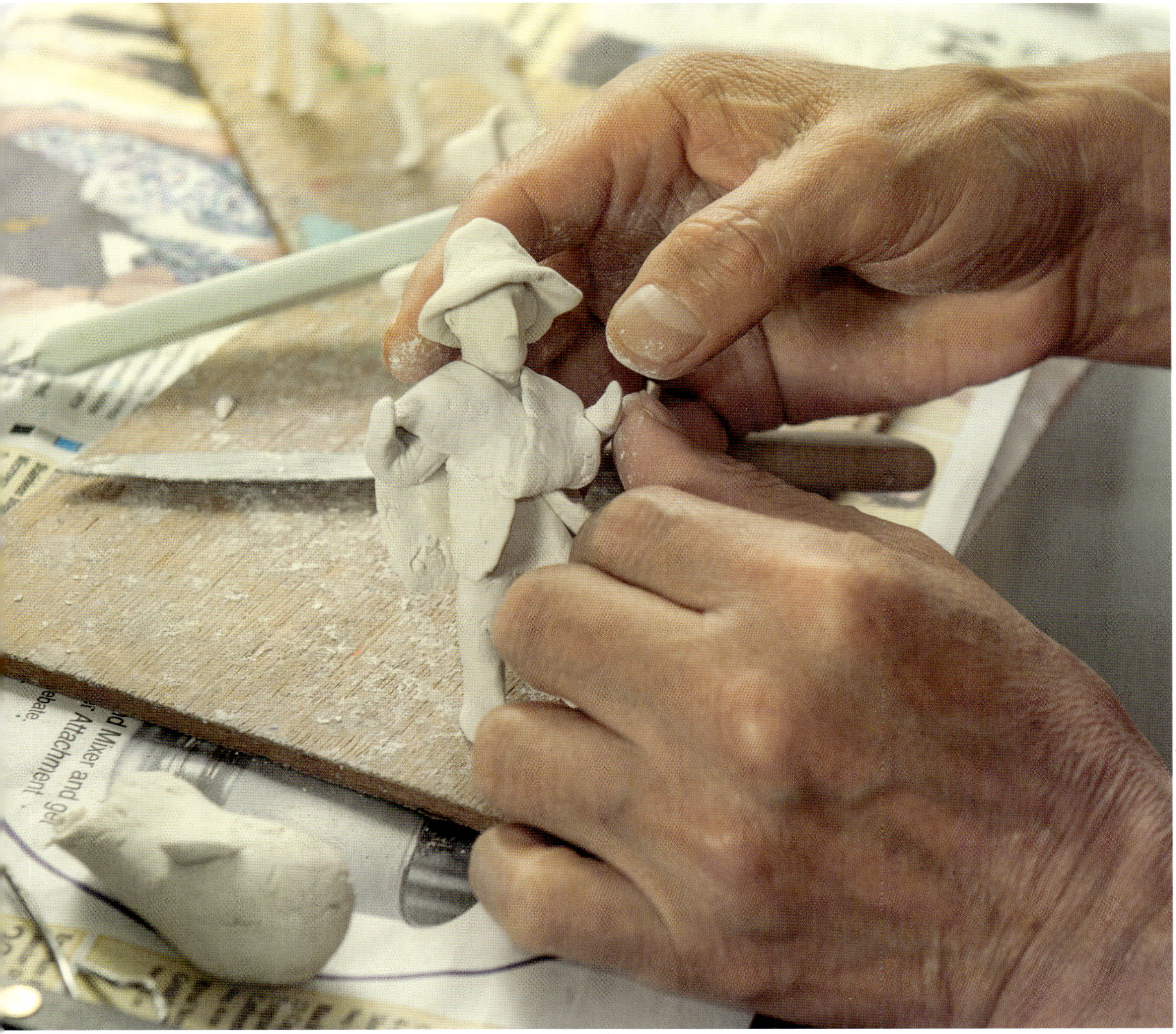

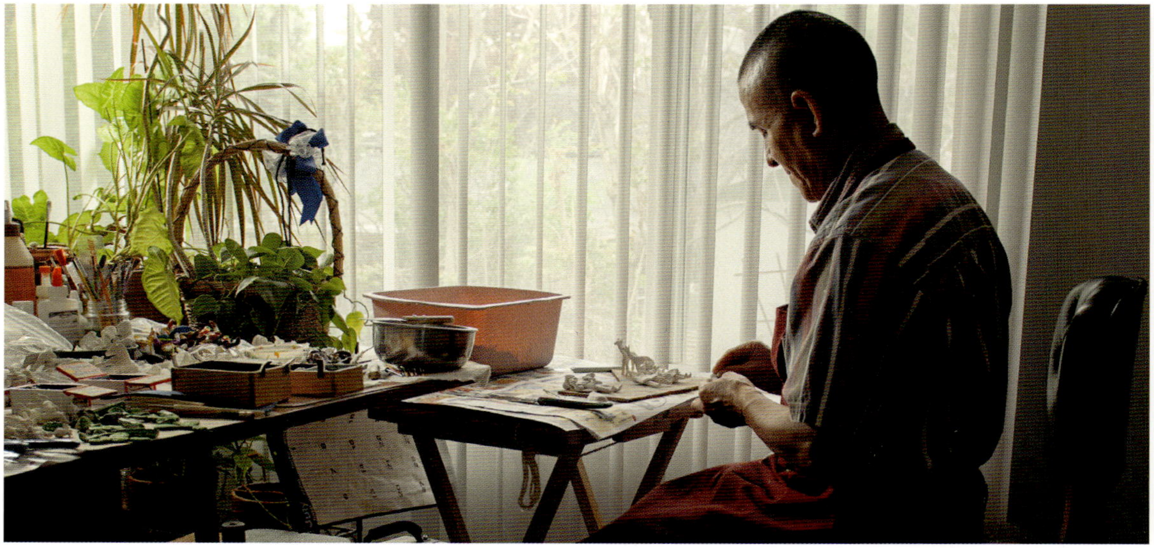

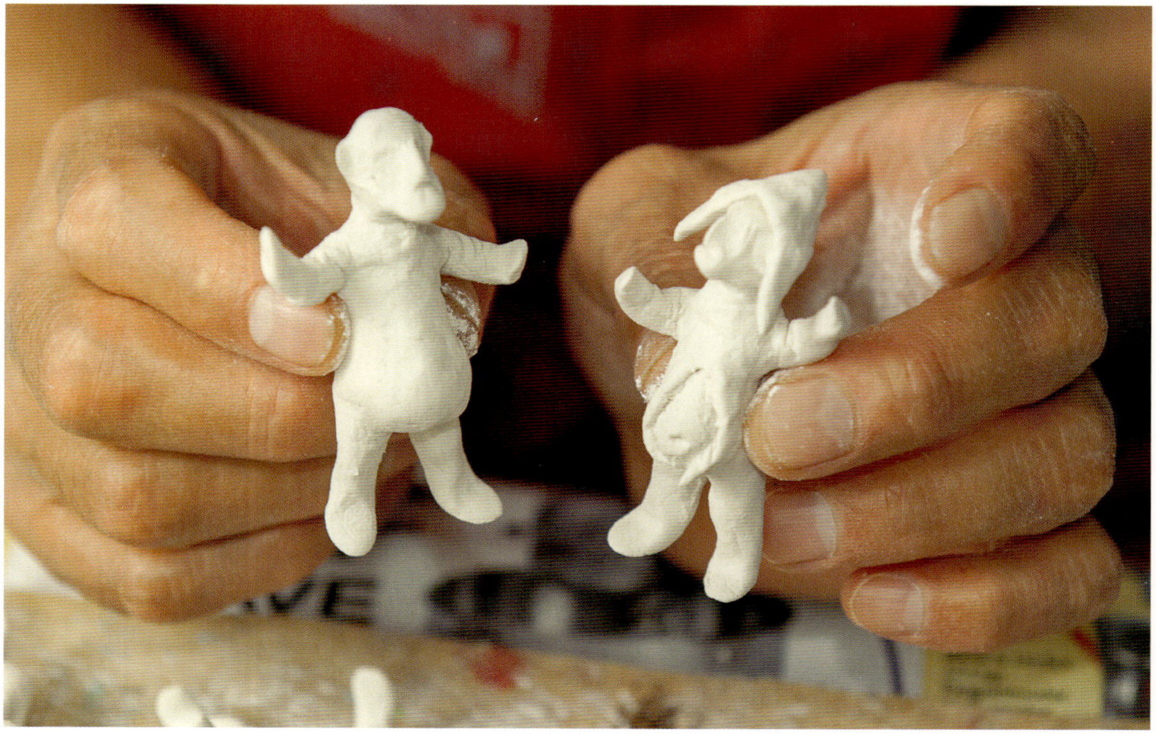

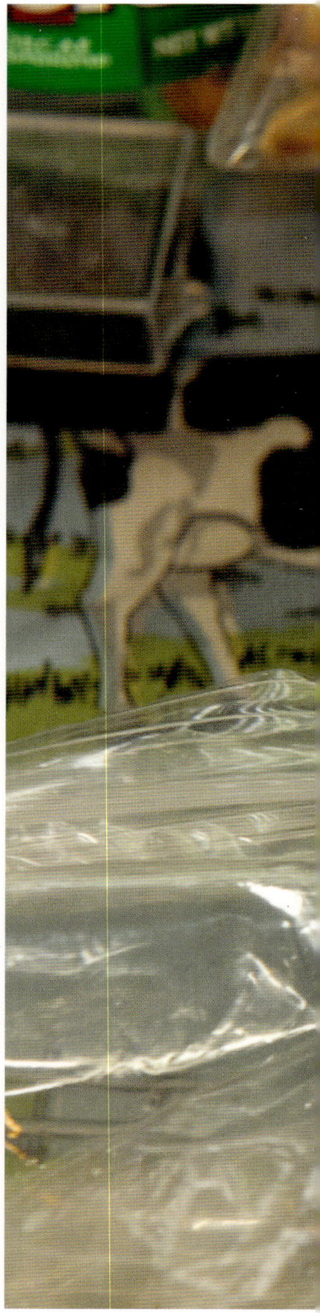

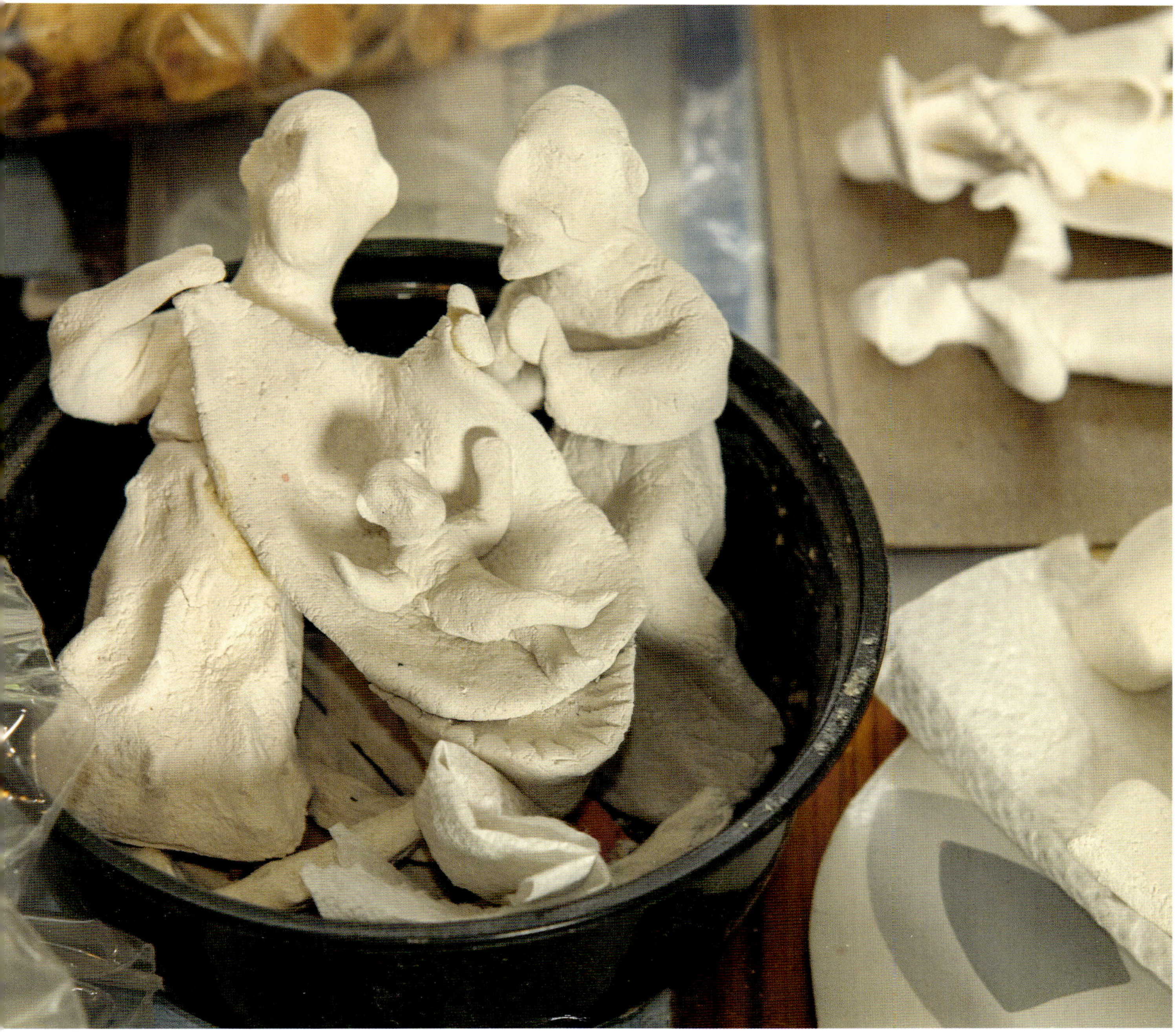

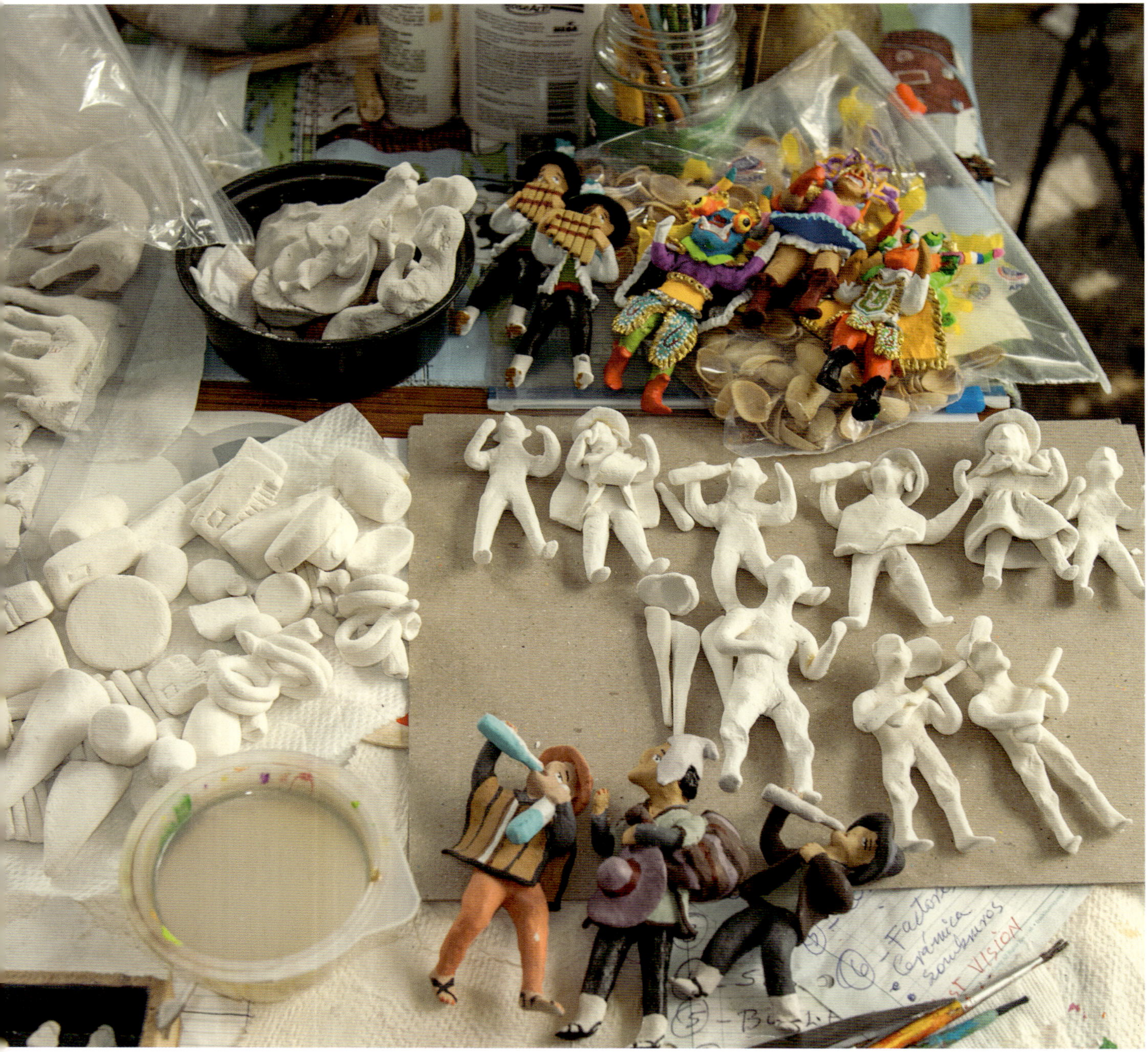

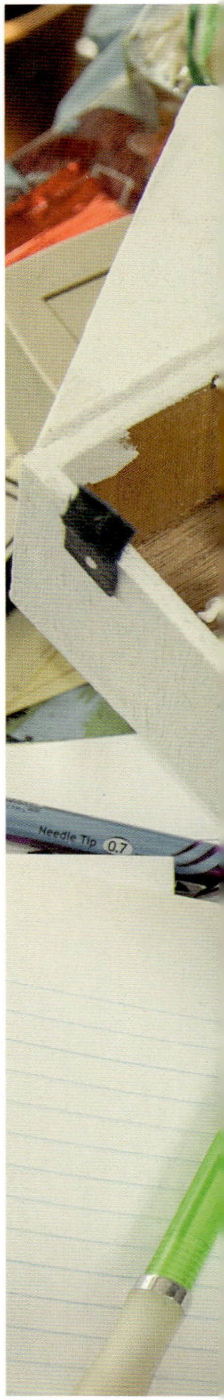
Needle Tip 0.7

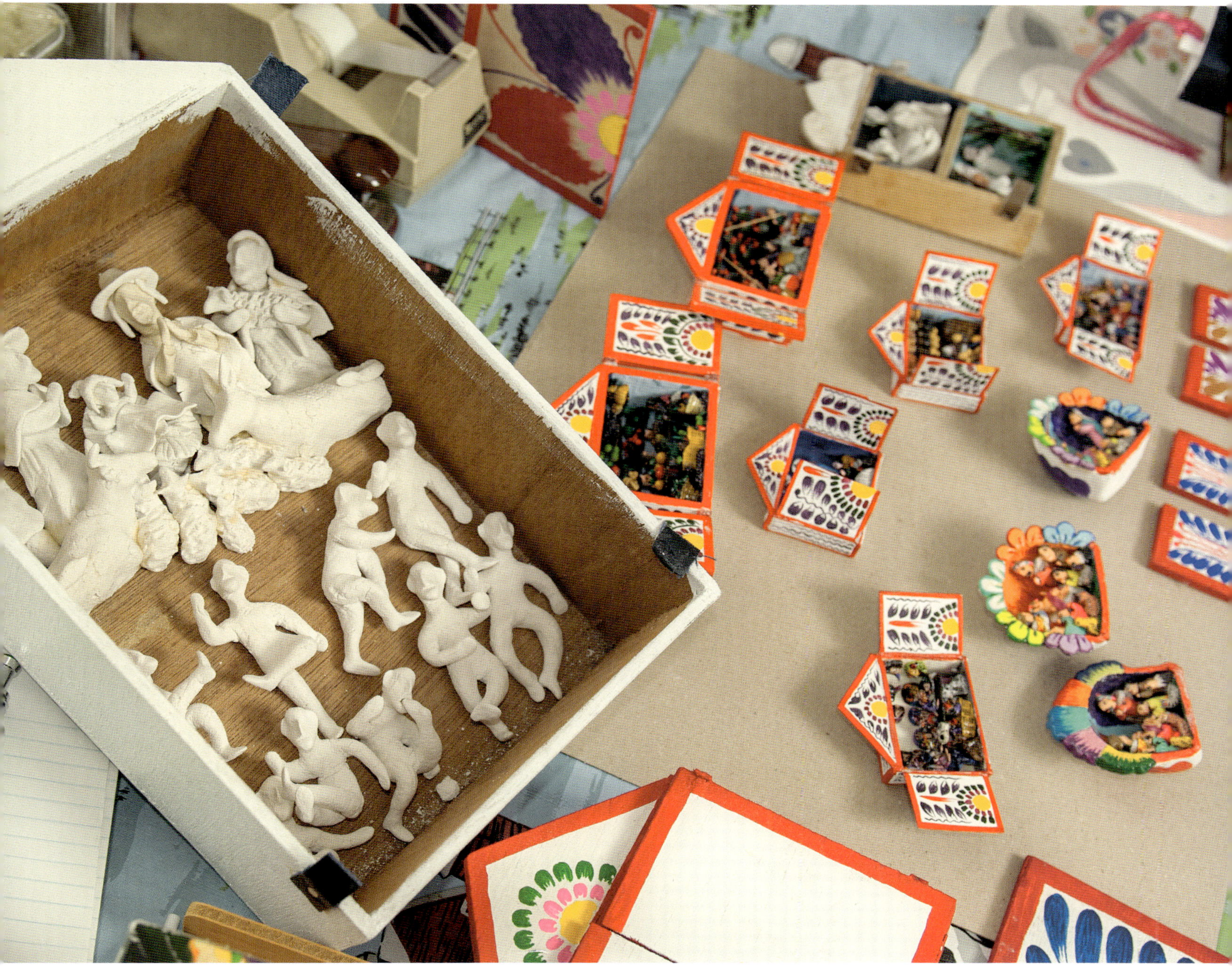

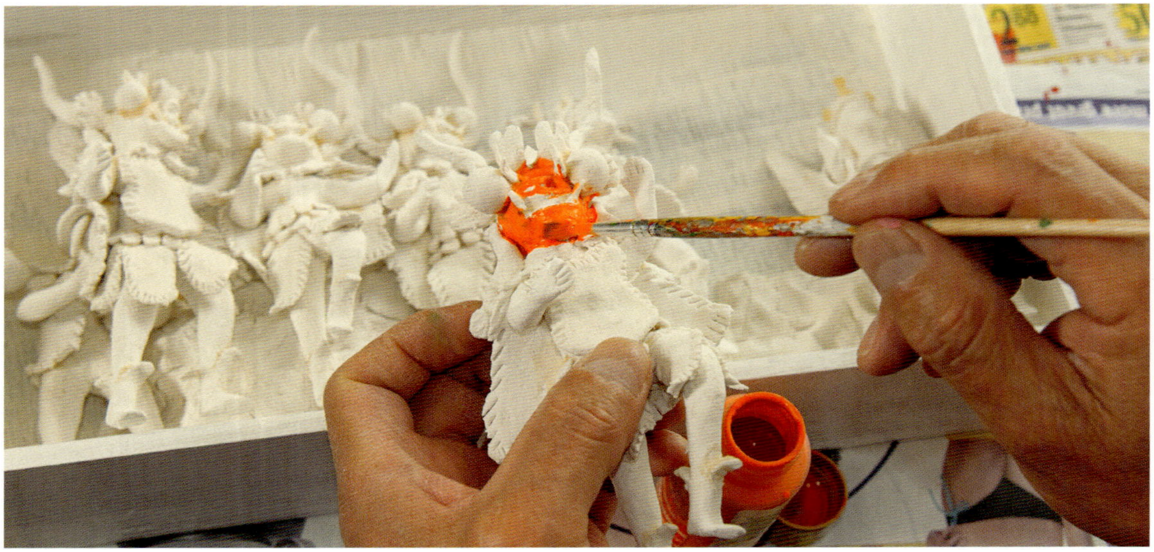

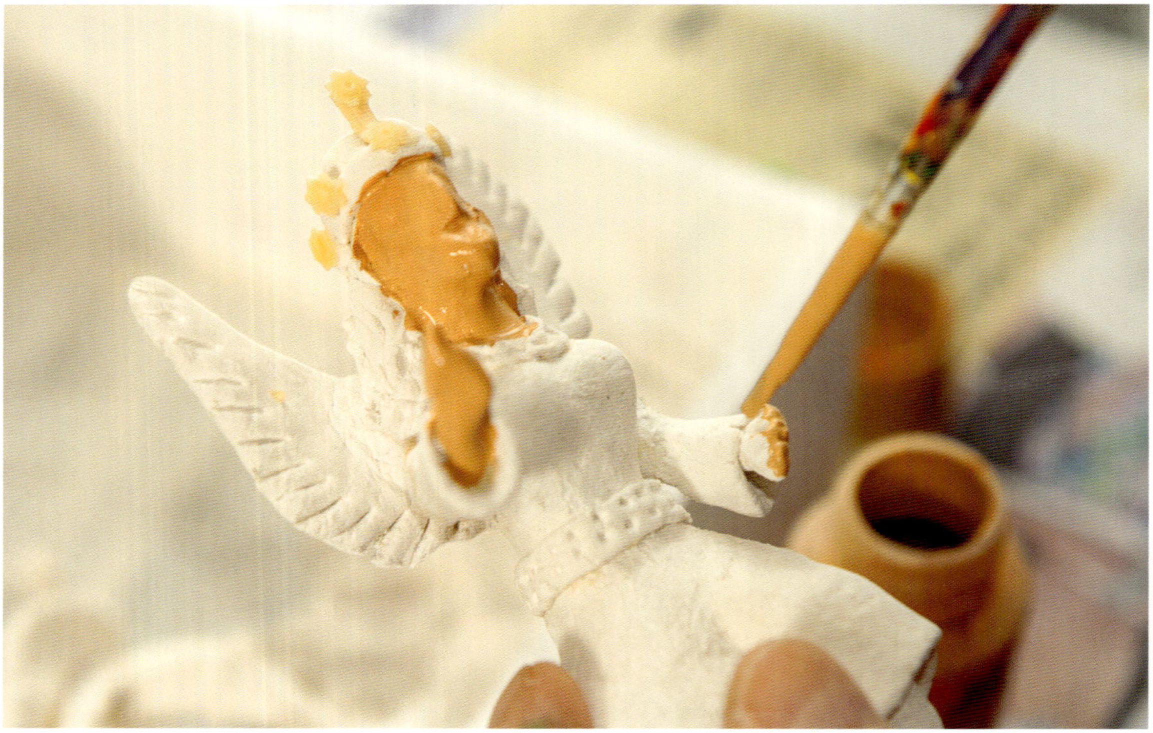

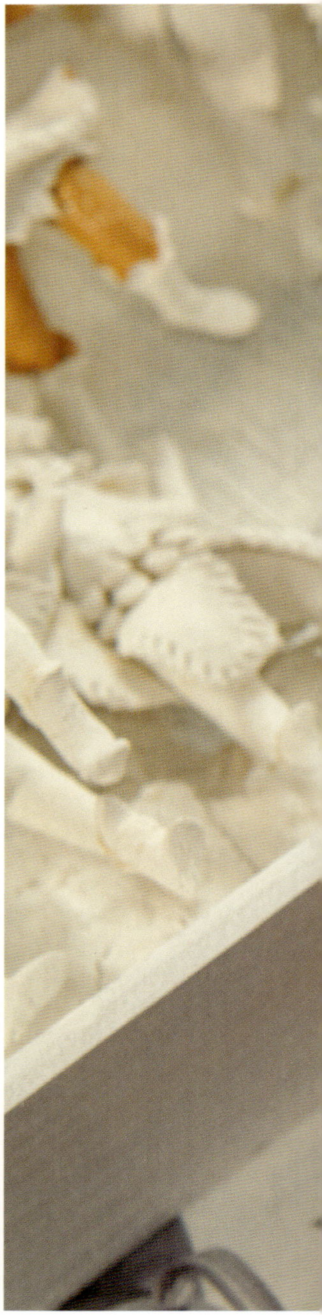

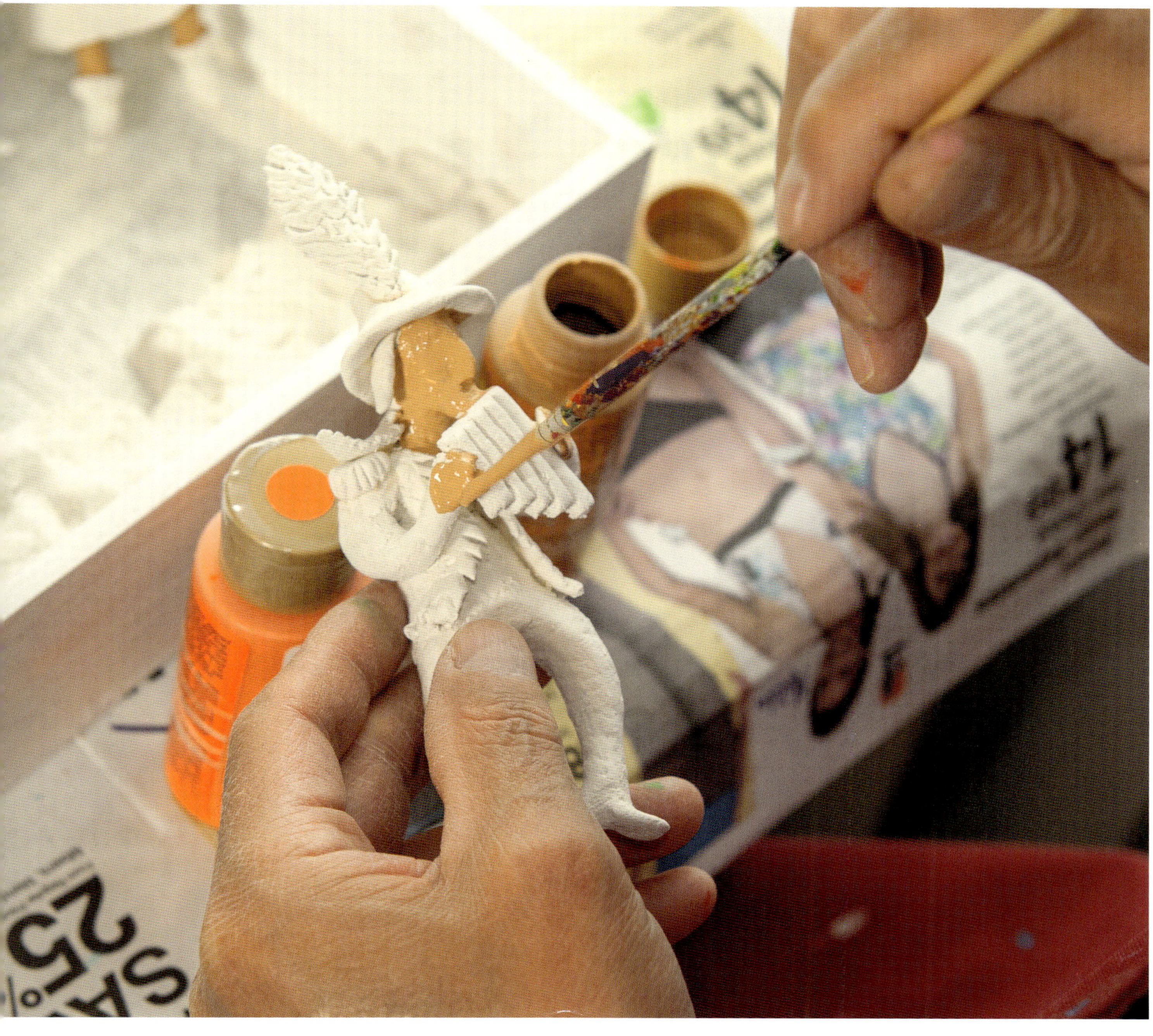

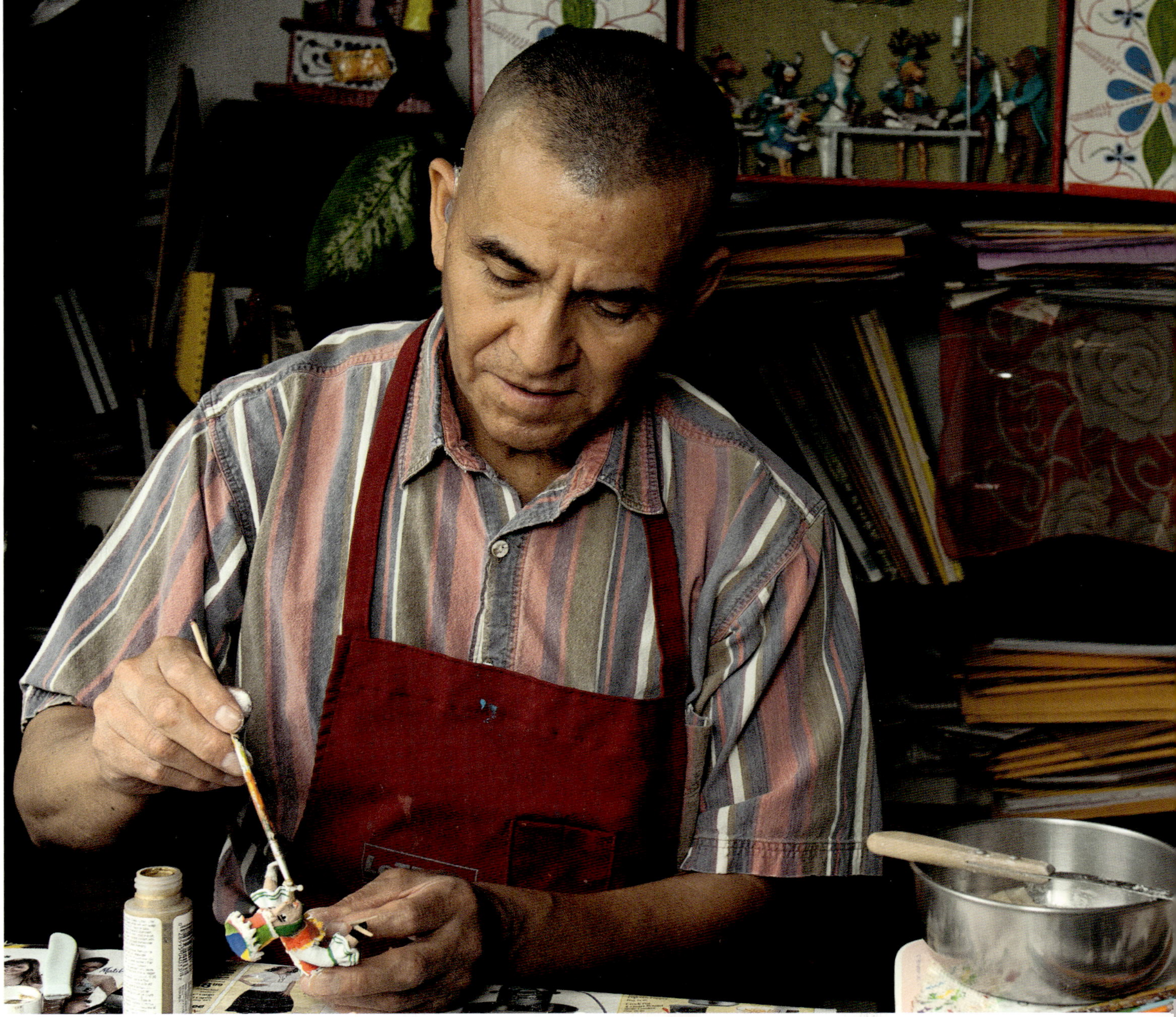

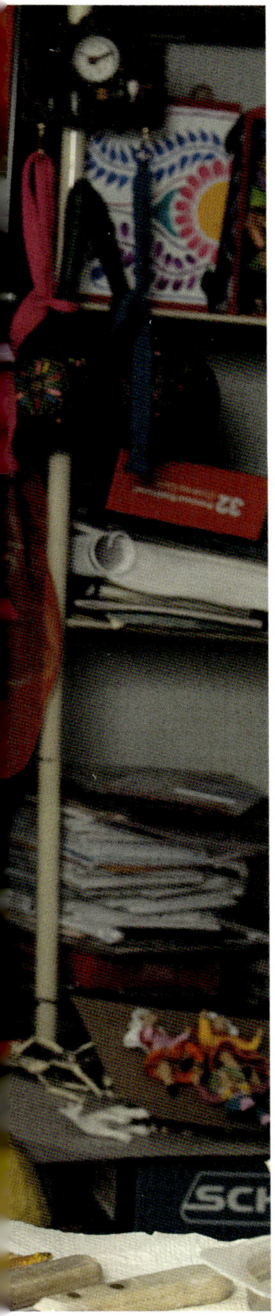

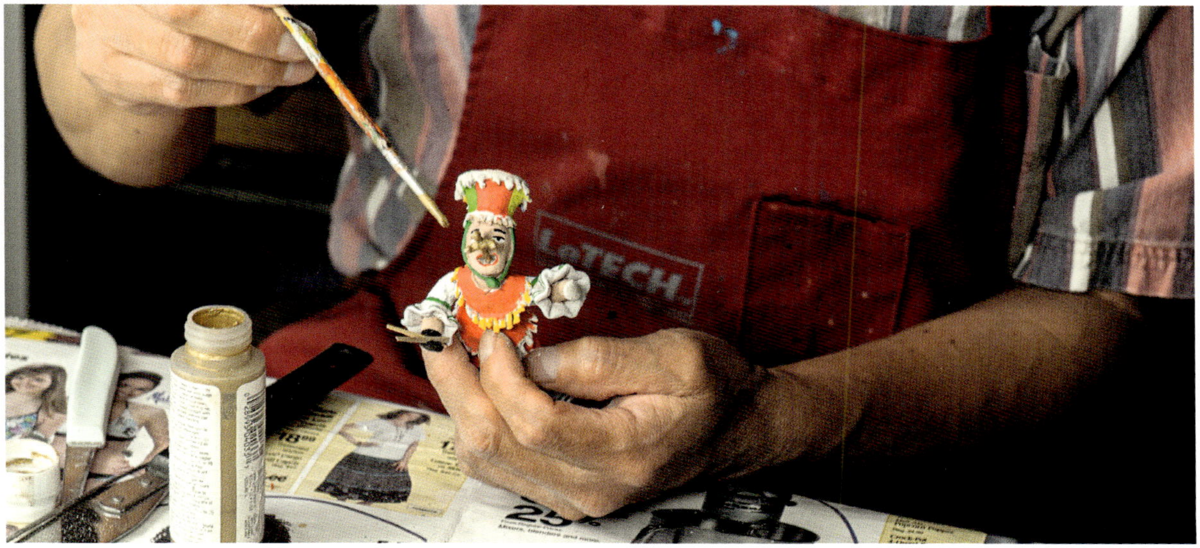

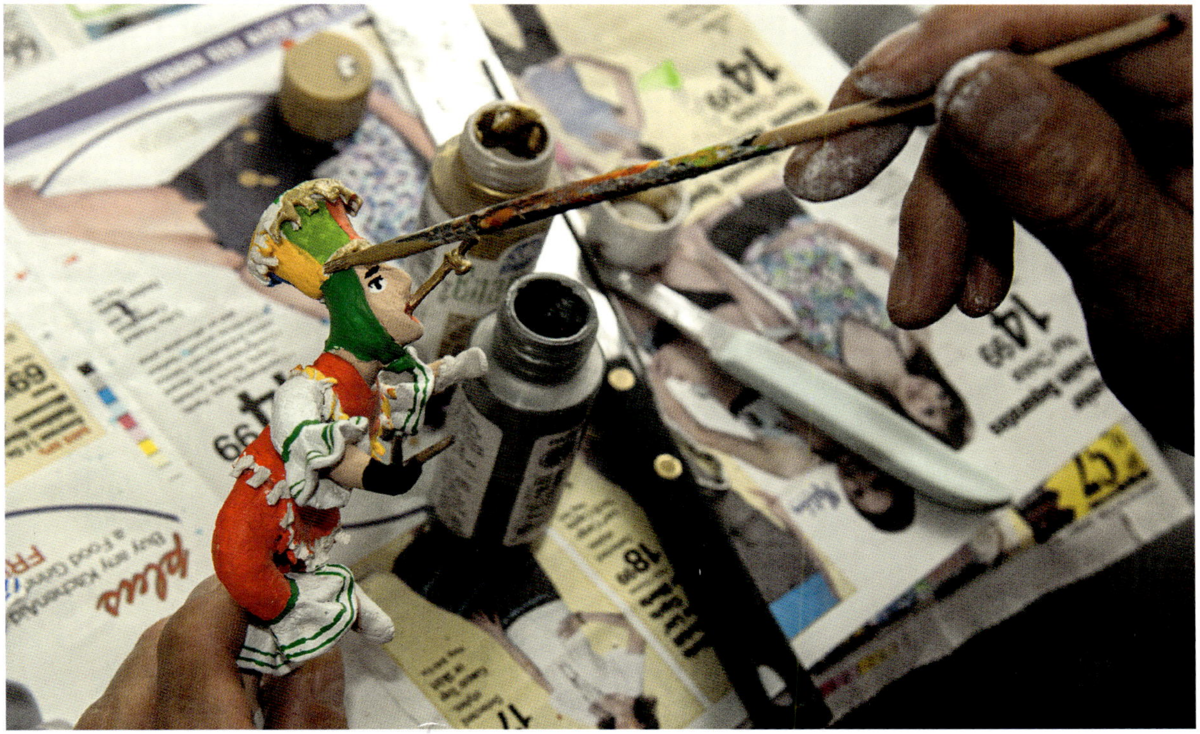

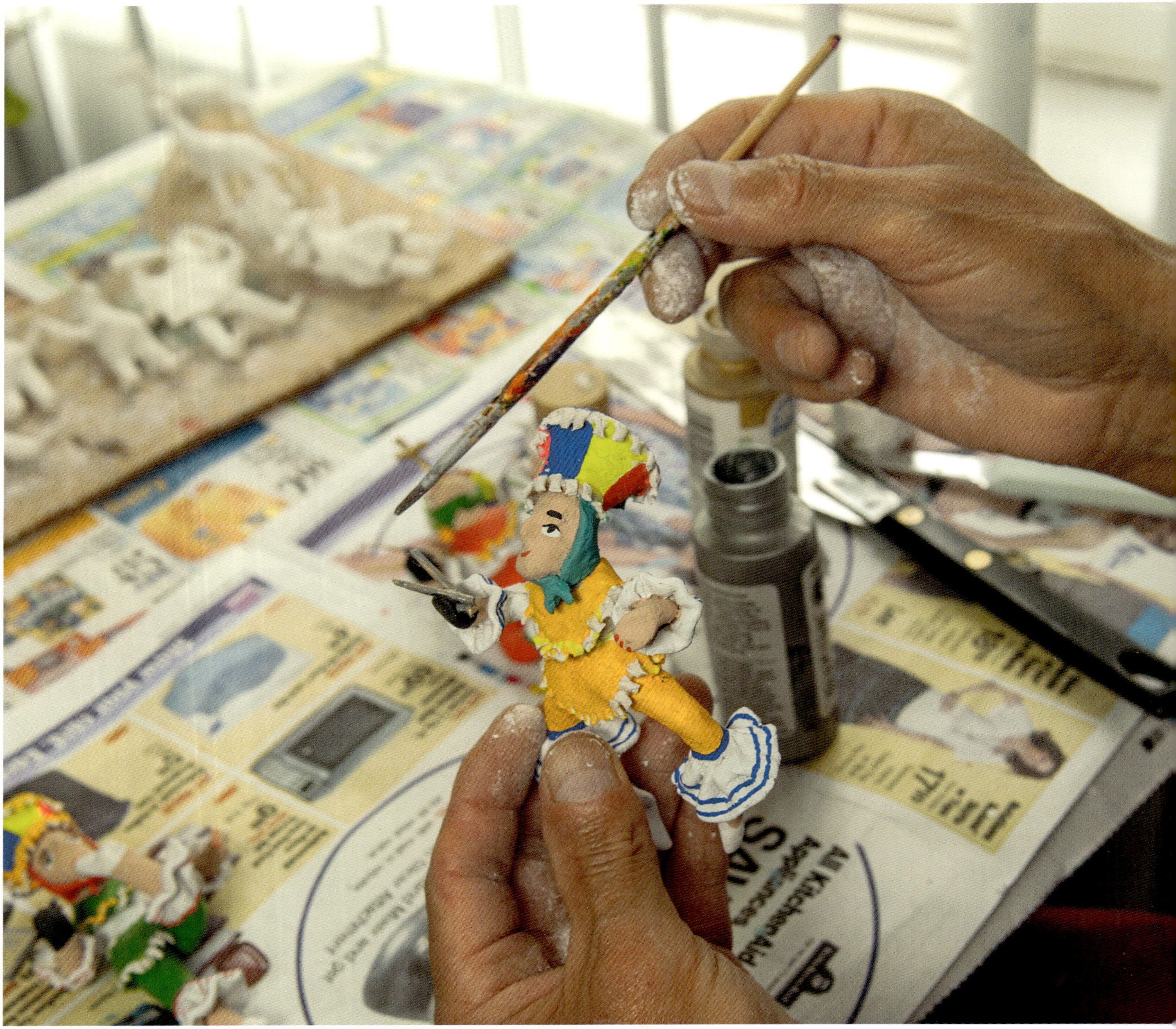

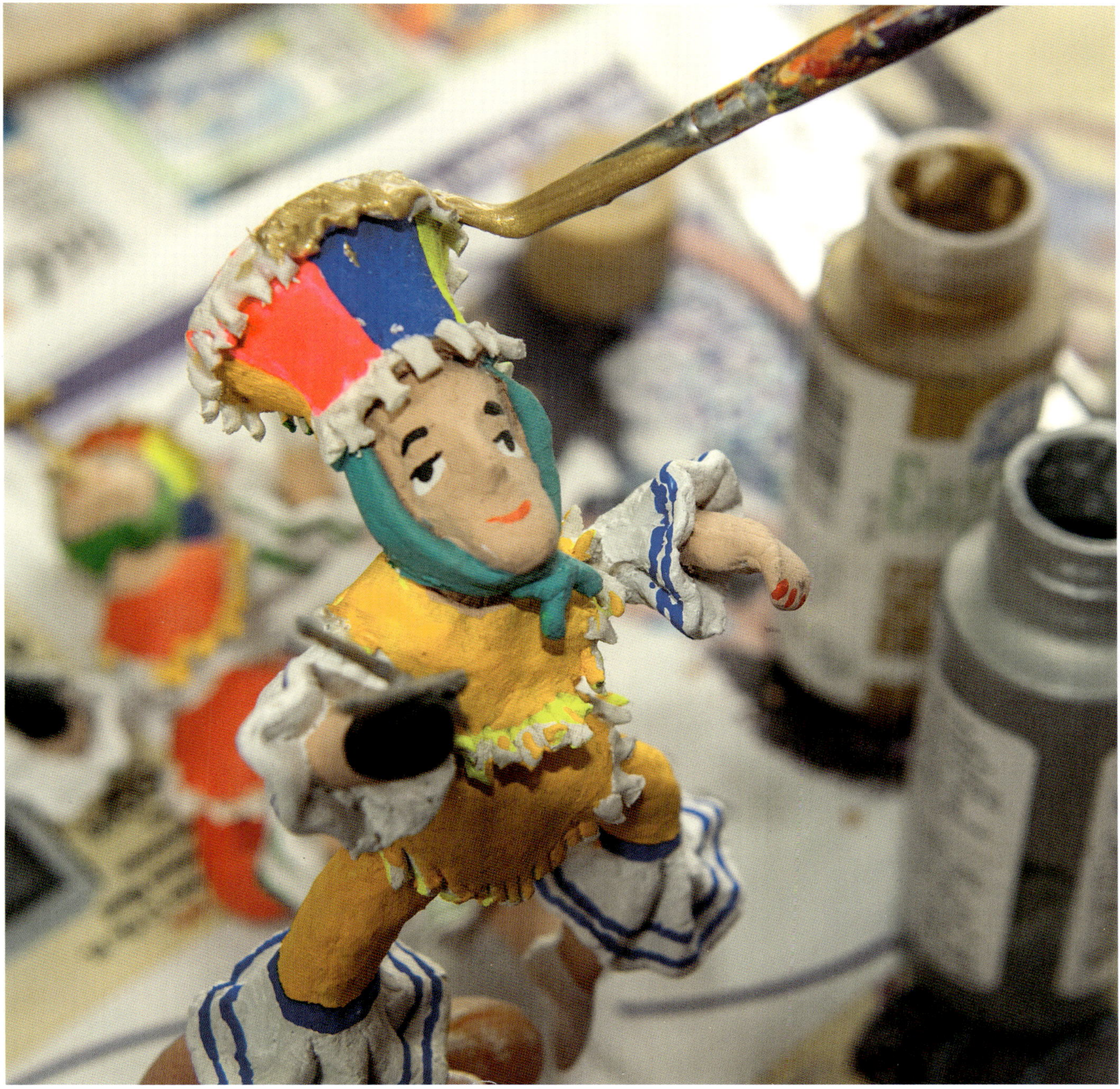

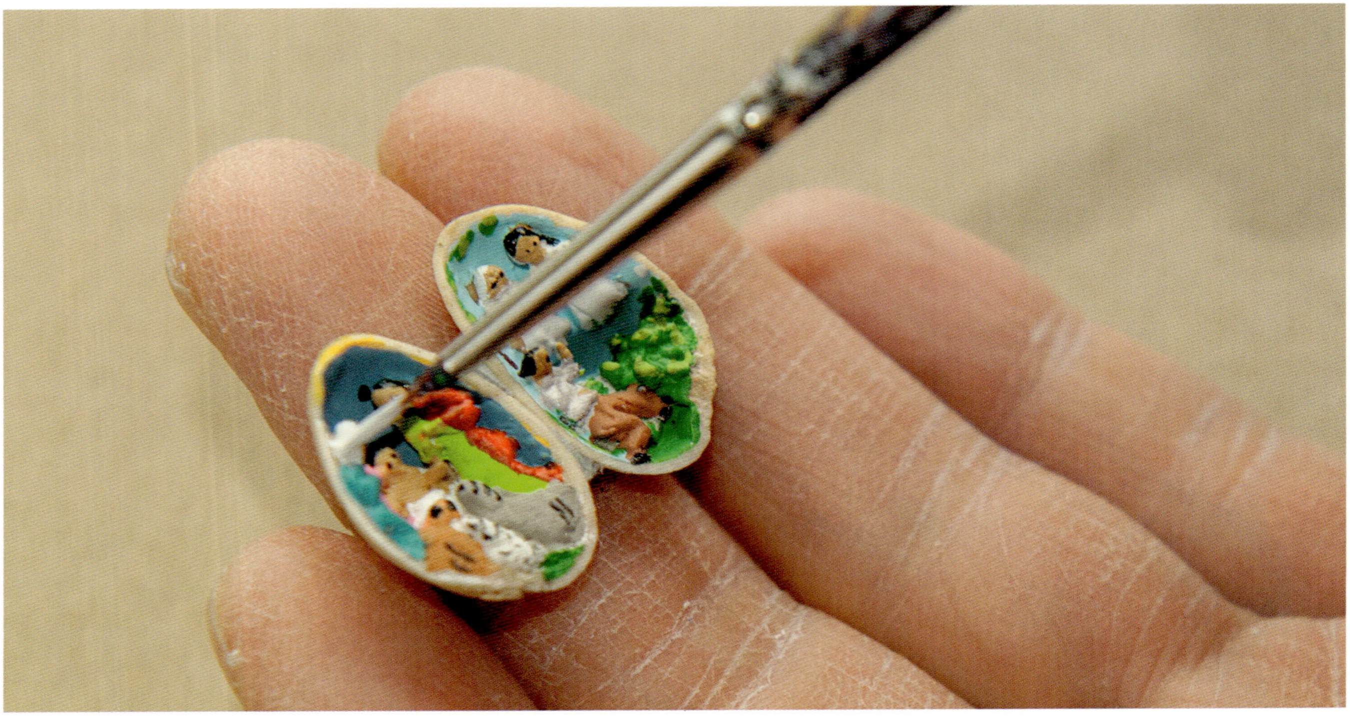

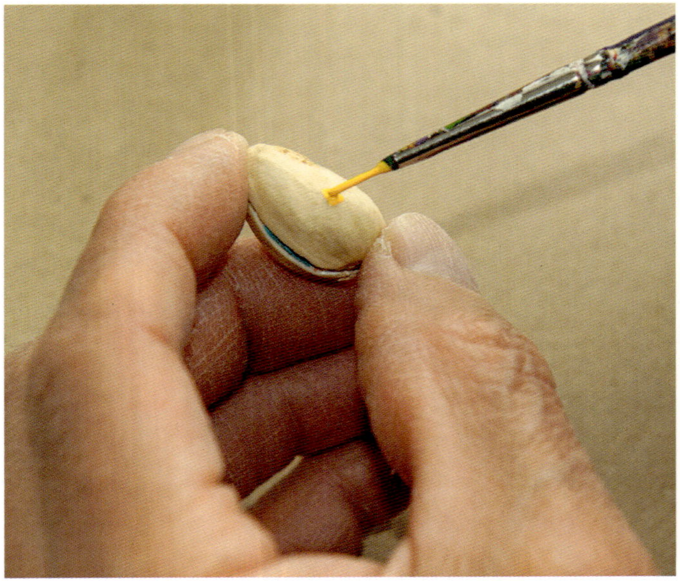

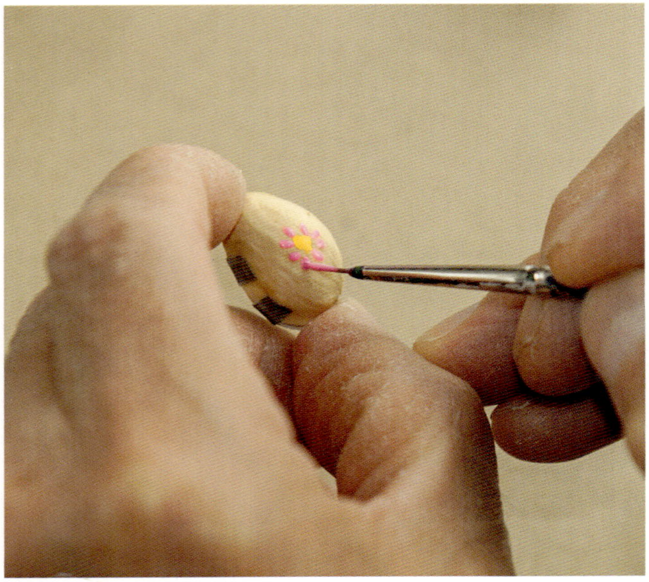

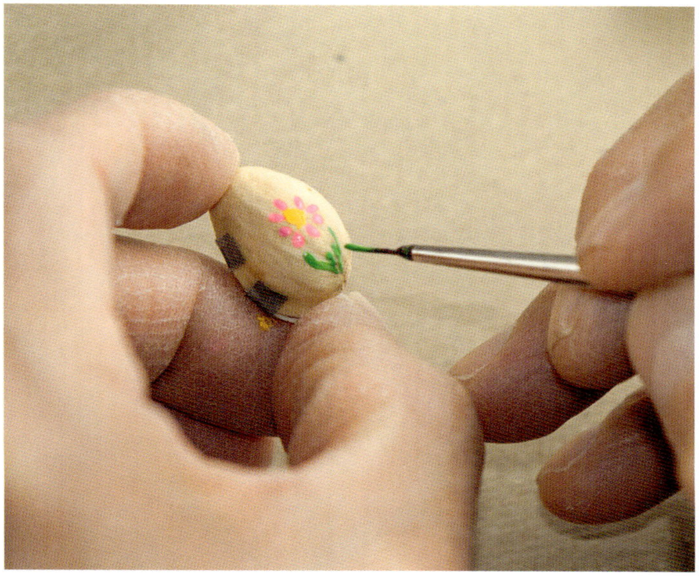

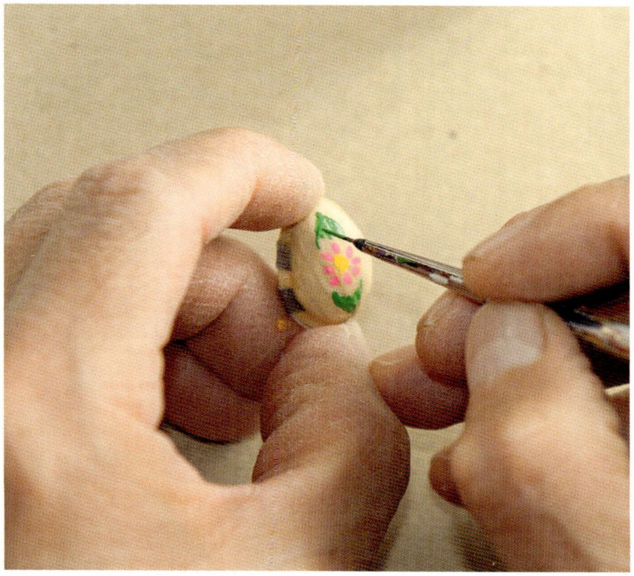

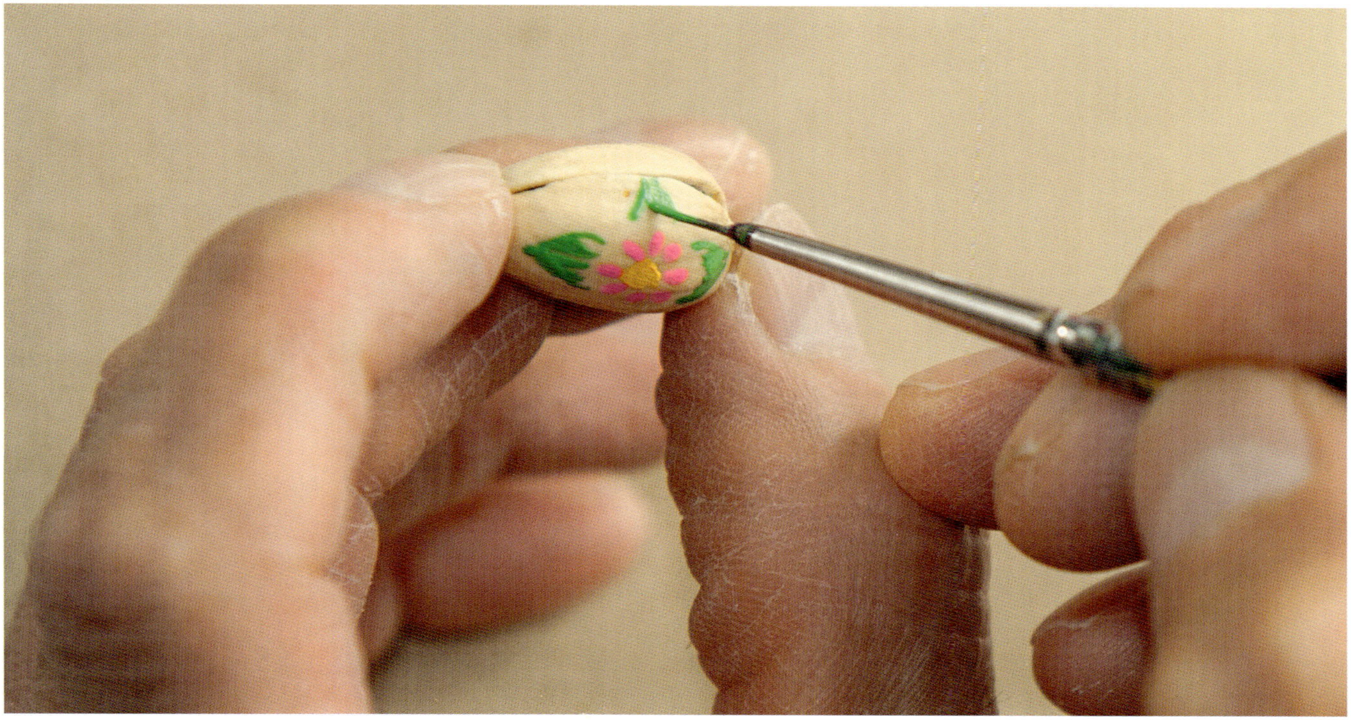

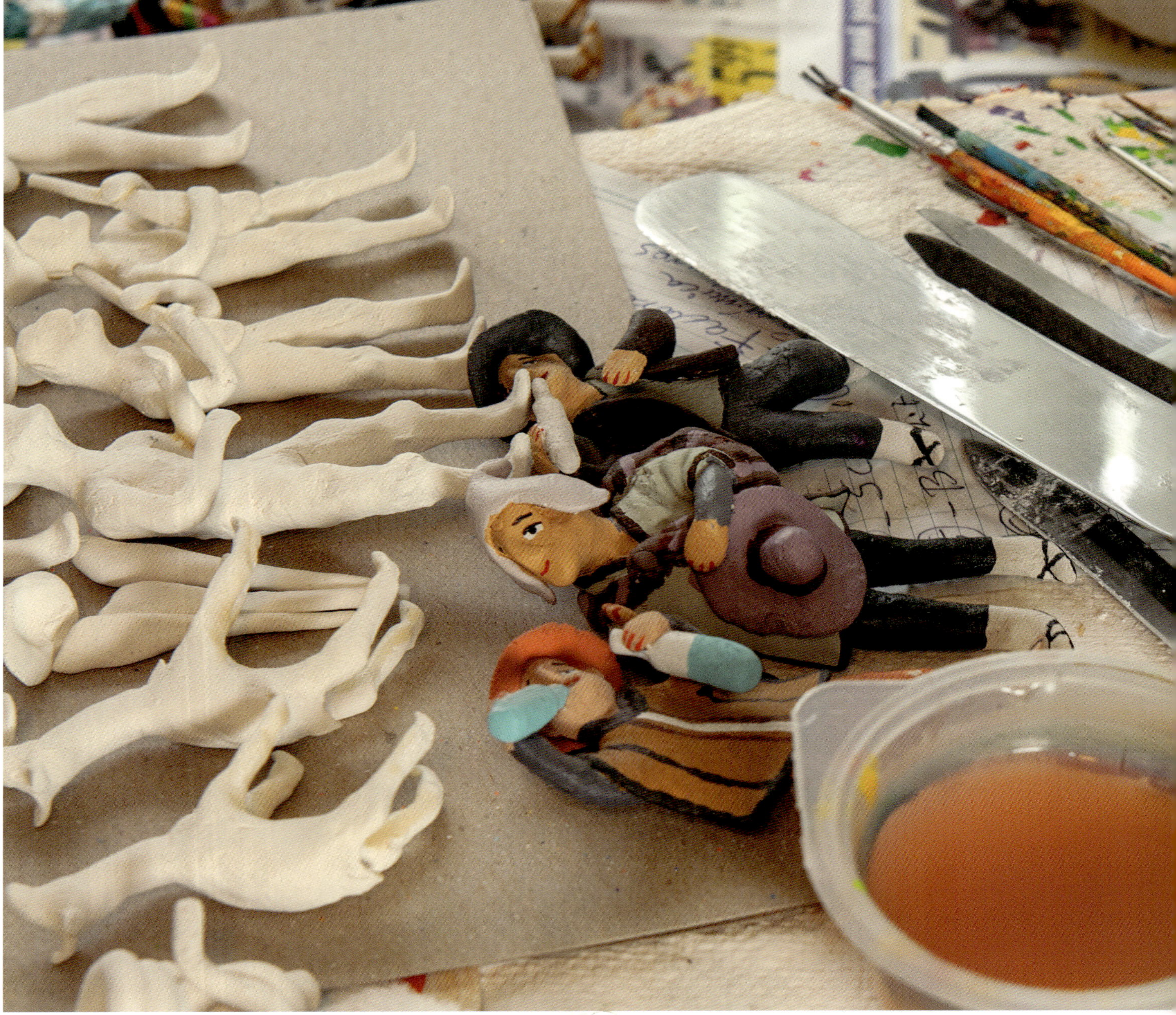

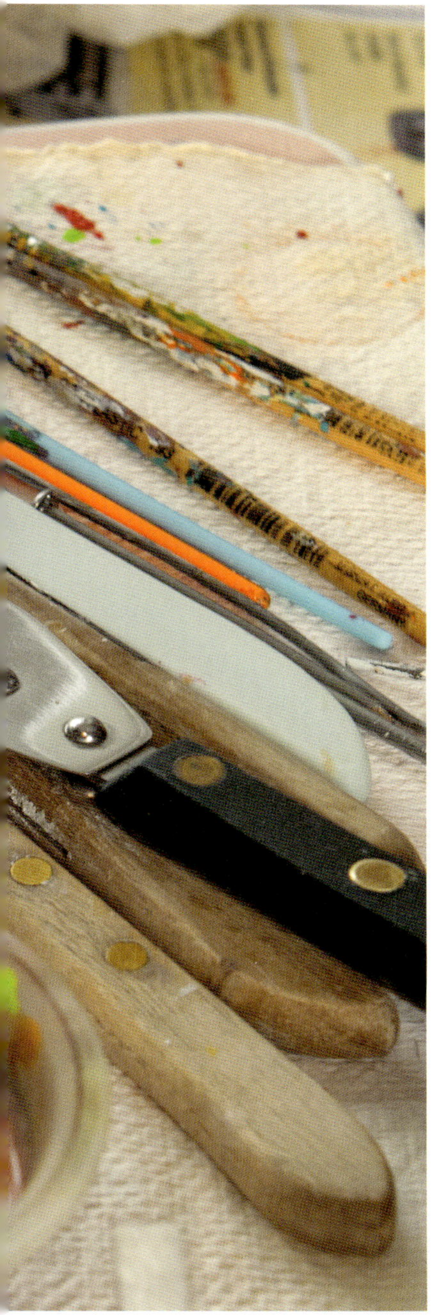

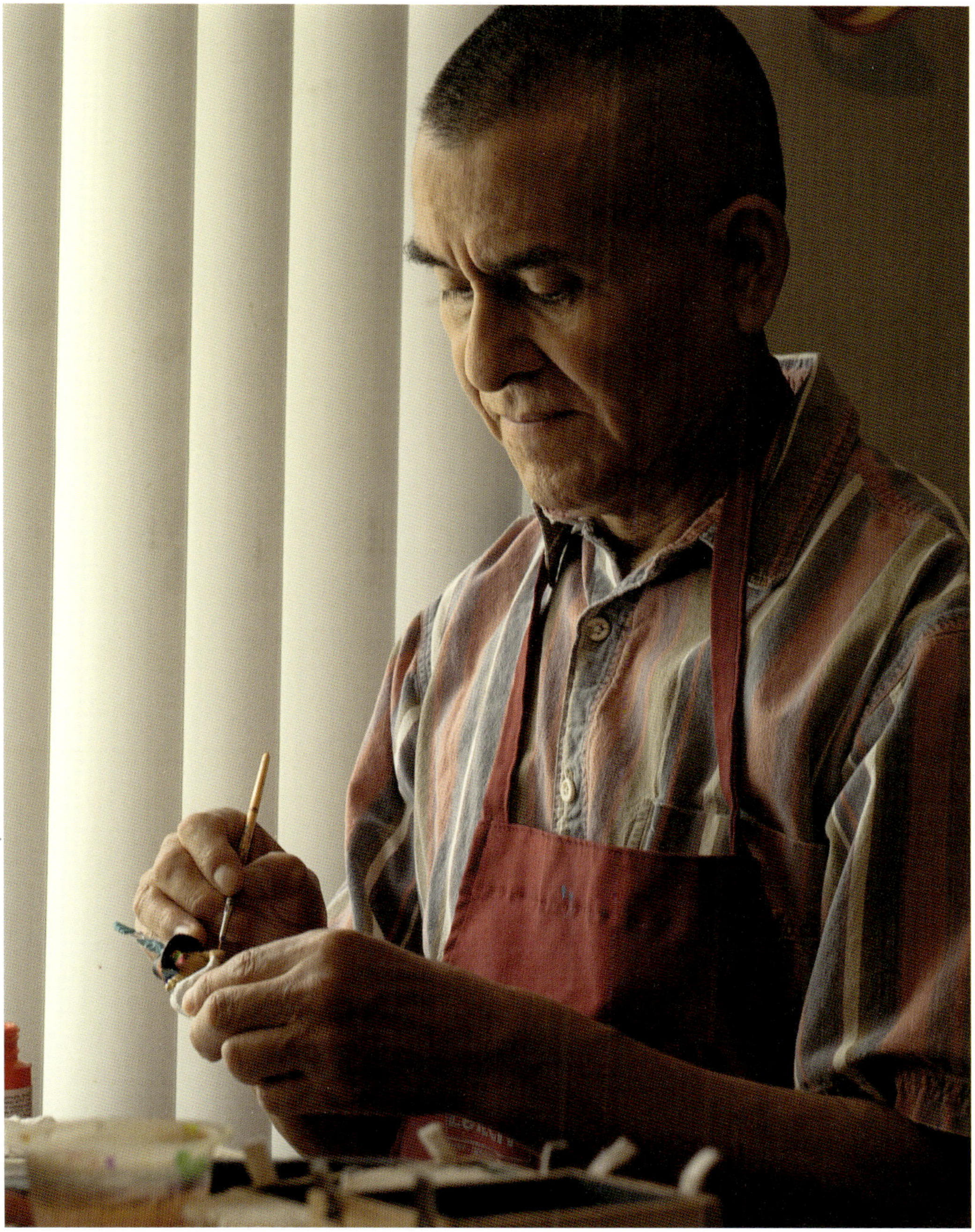

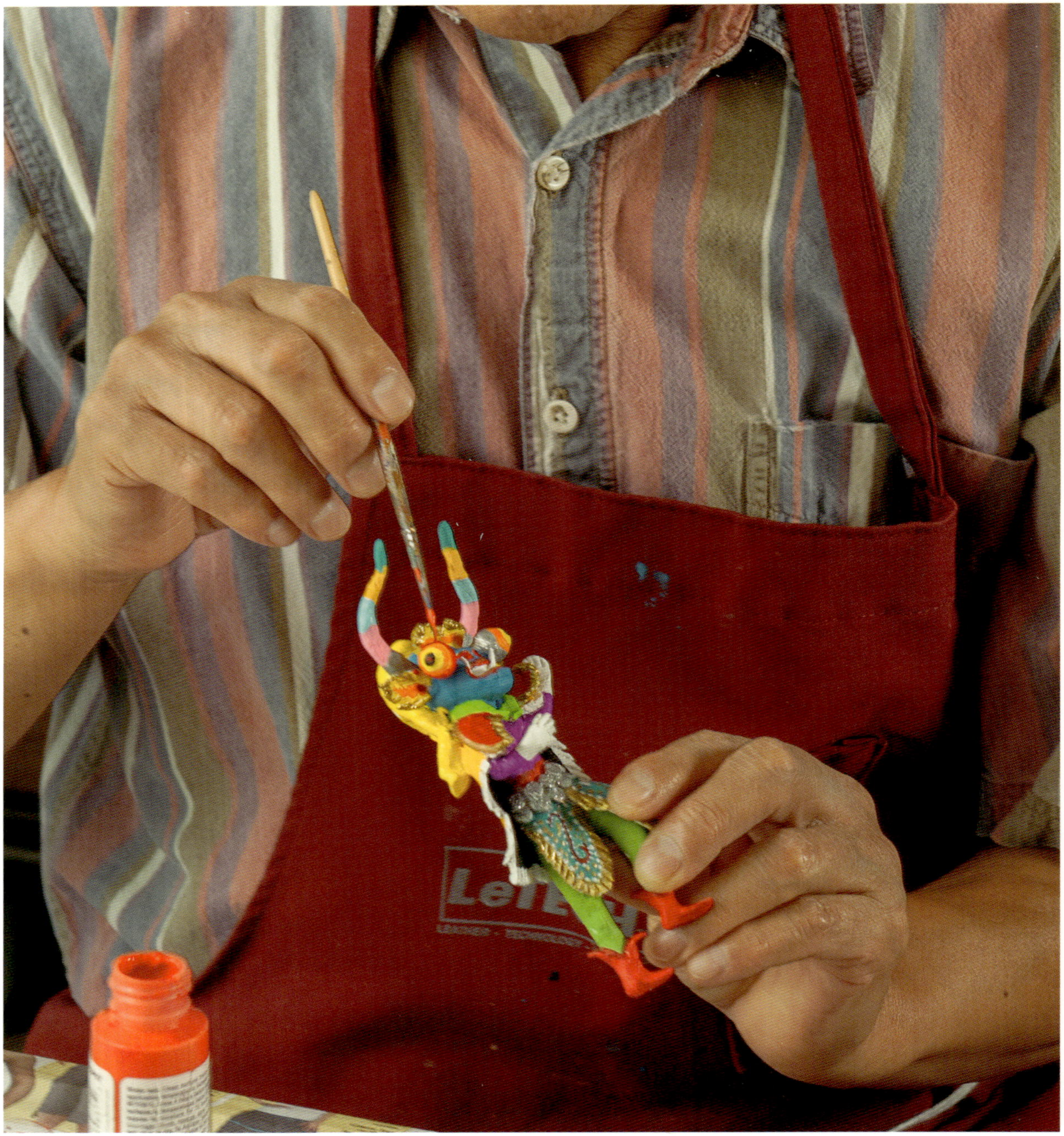

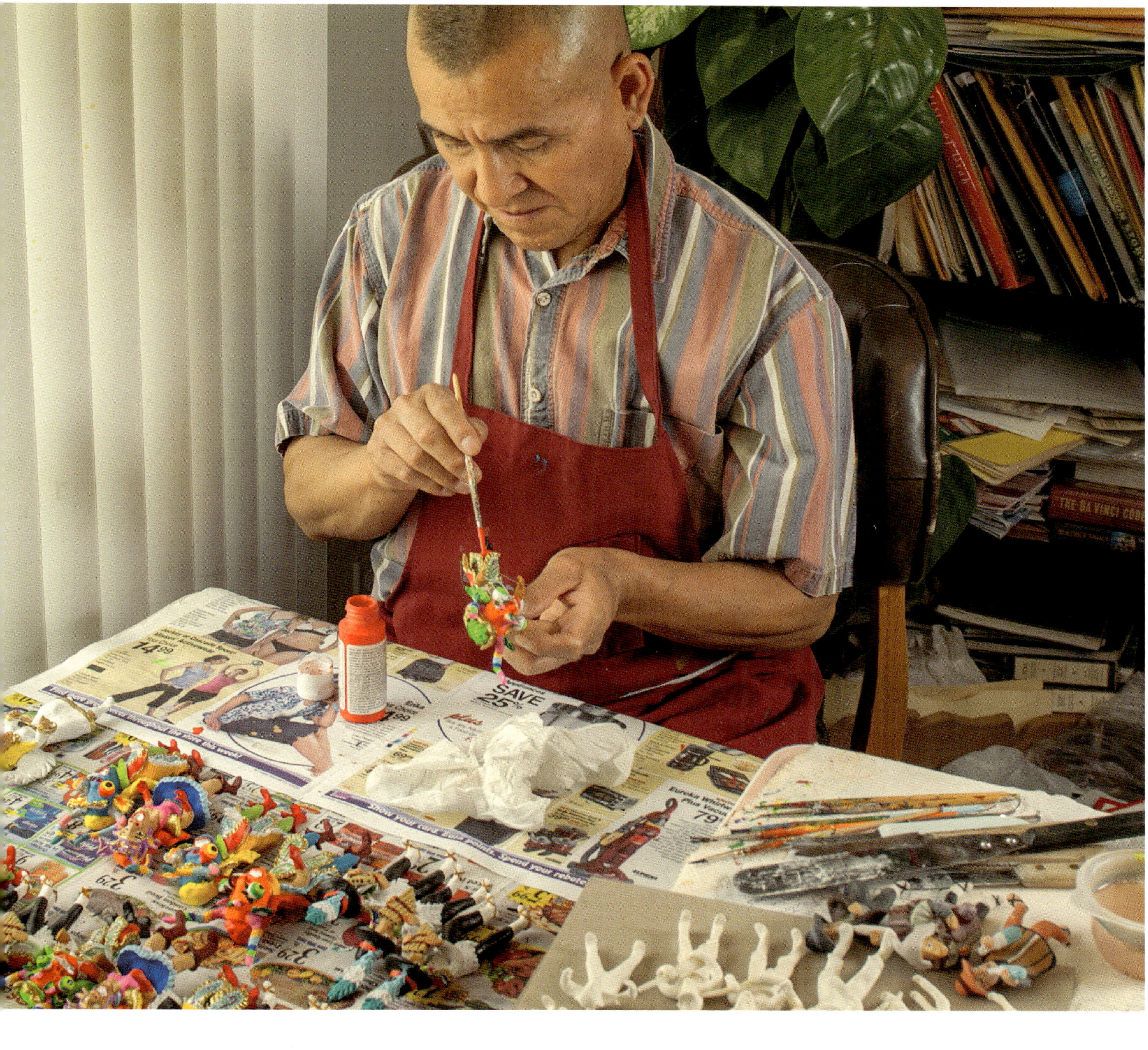
SAVE
25%

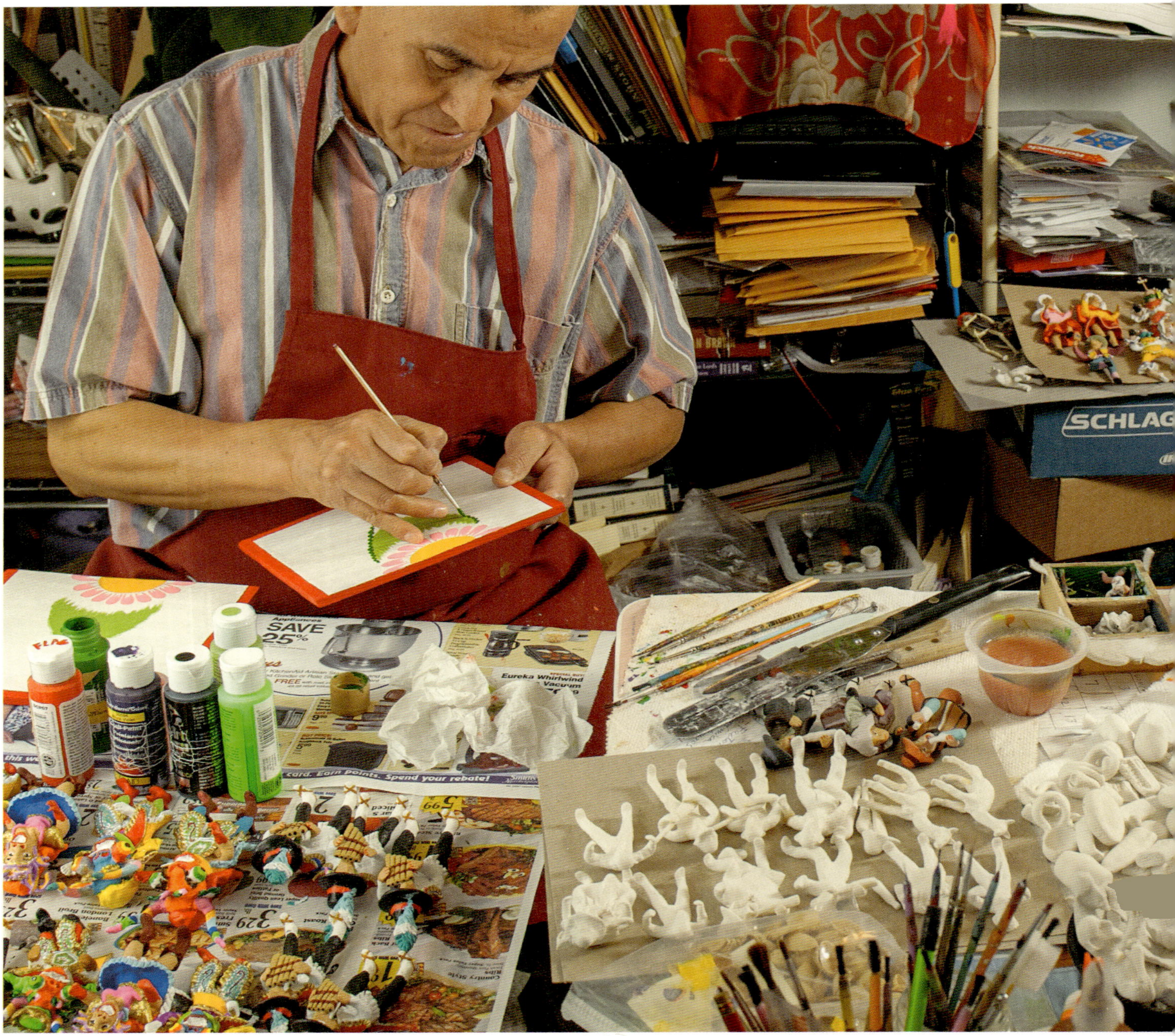
SAVE
25%
Eureka Whirlwind
card. Earn points. Spend your rebate!
SCHLAG

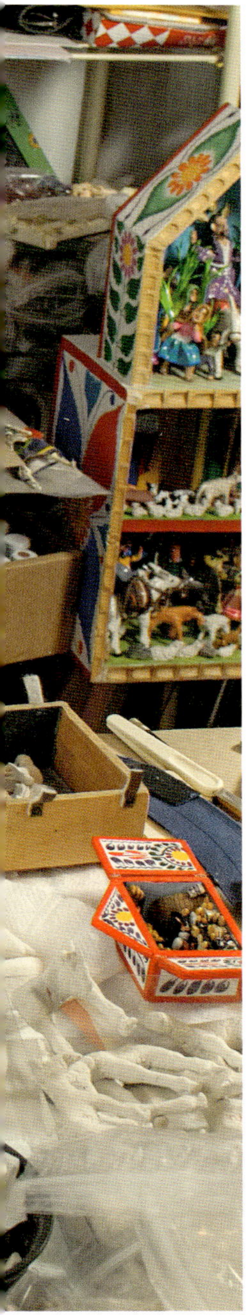

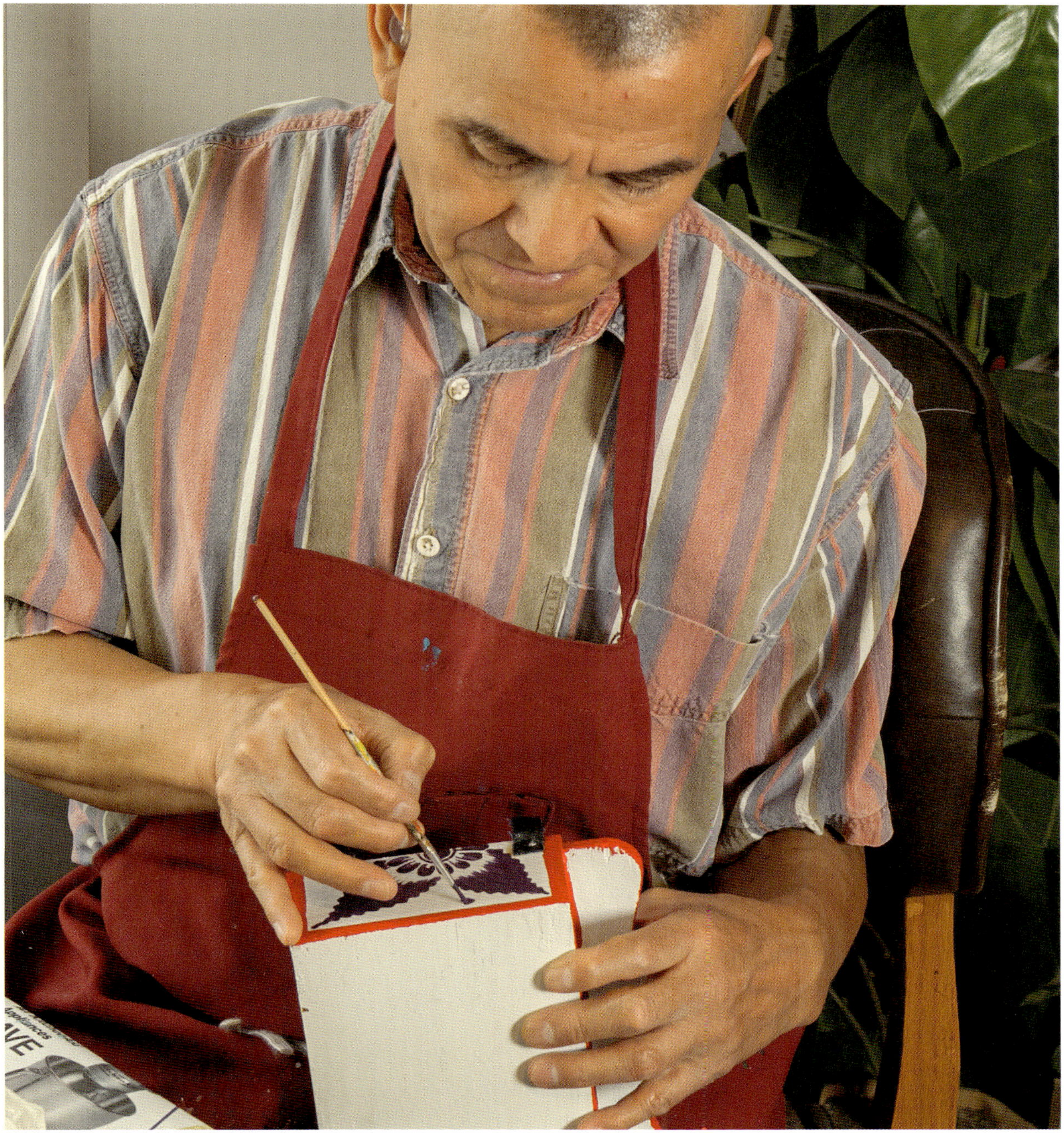

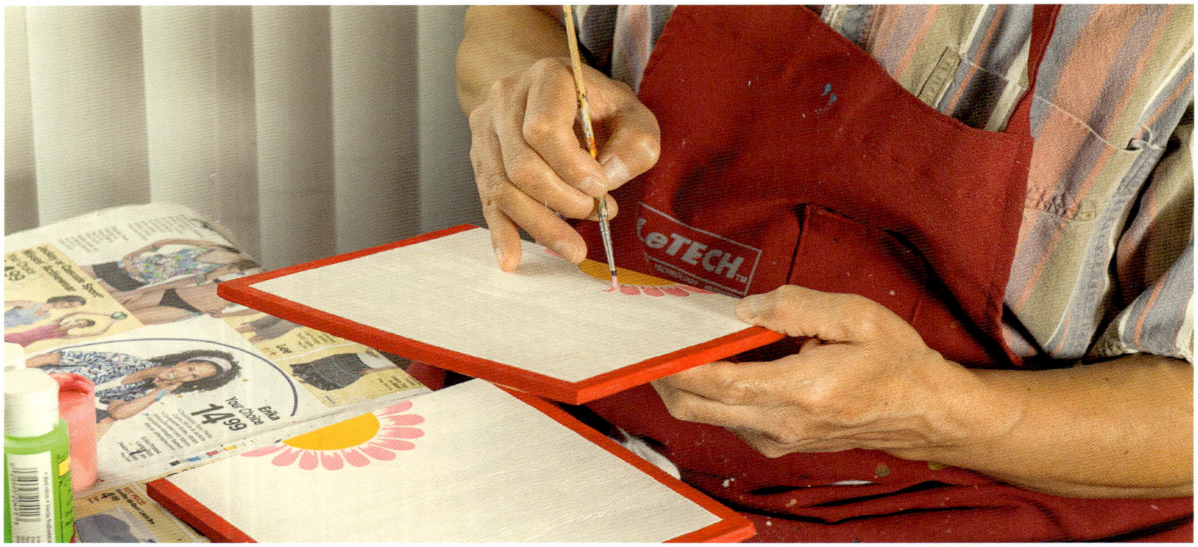

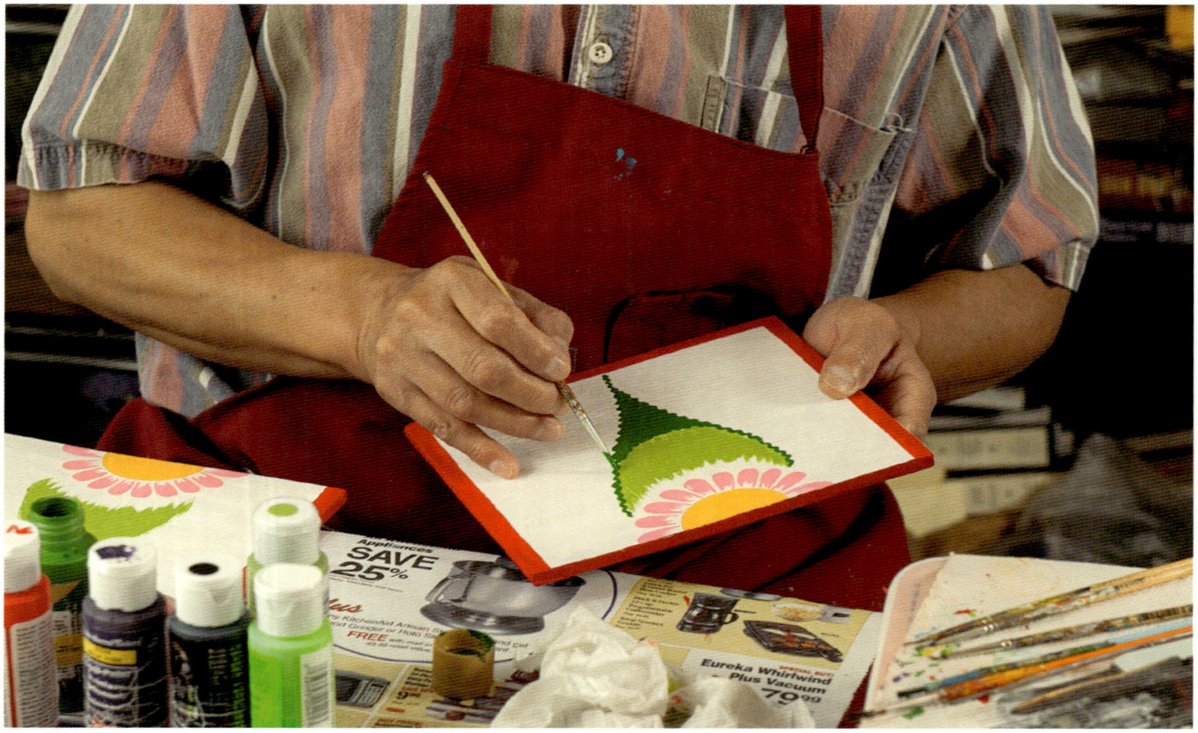
Appliances
SAVE
25%
FREE
Eureka Whirlwind
Plus Vacuum

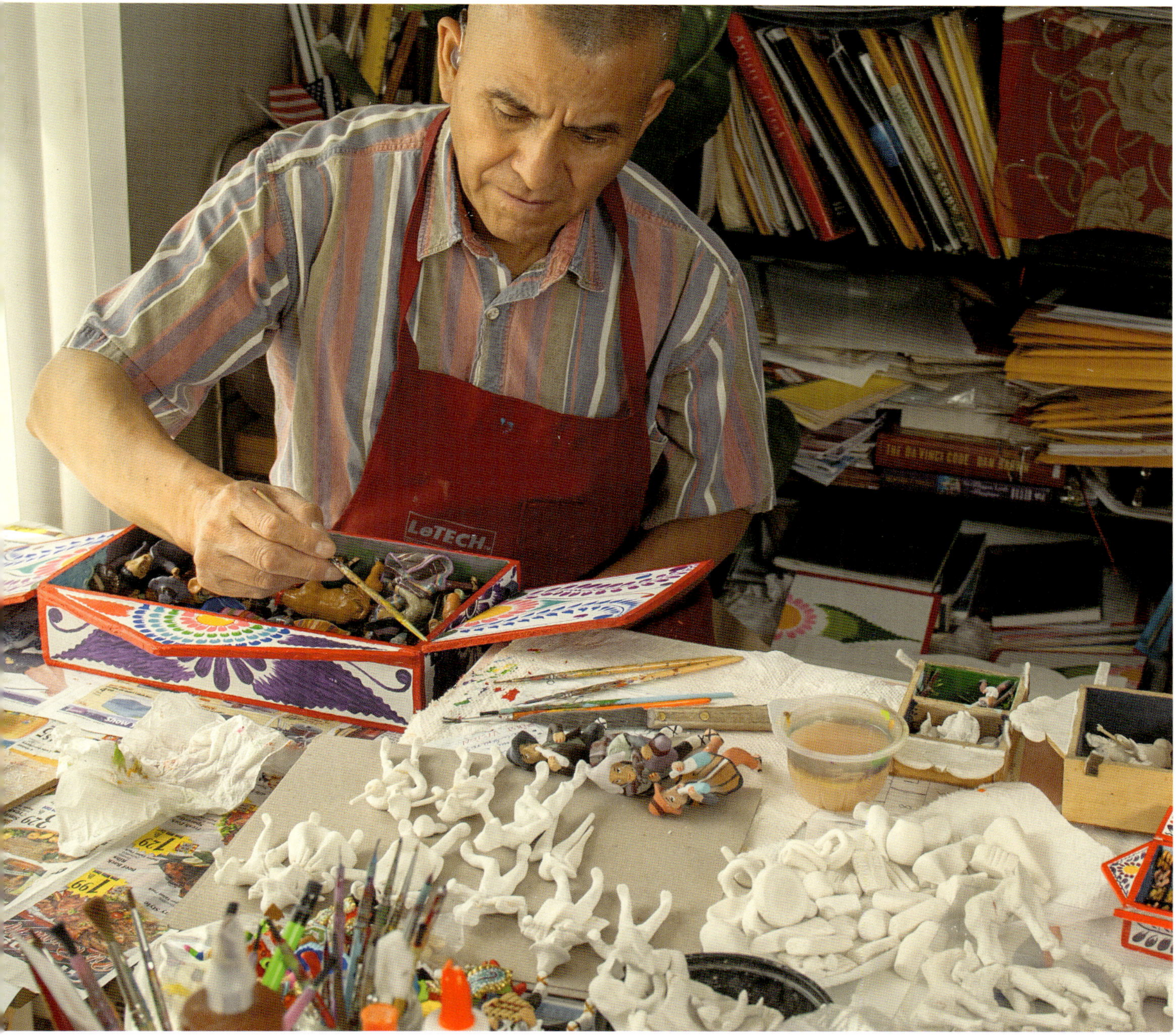

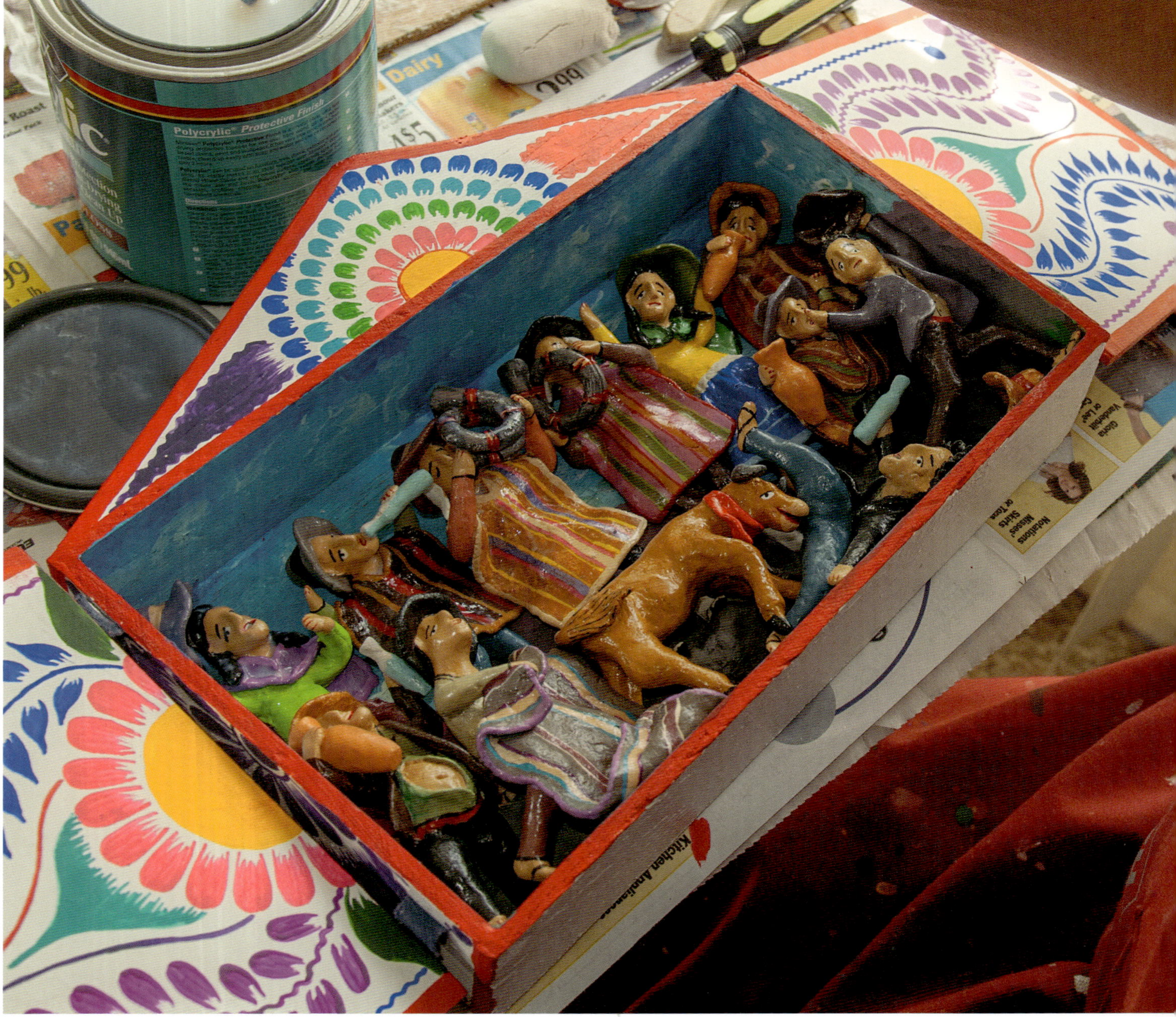
Polycrylic™ Protective Finish
Dairy

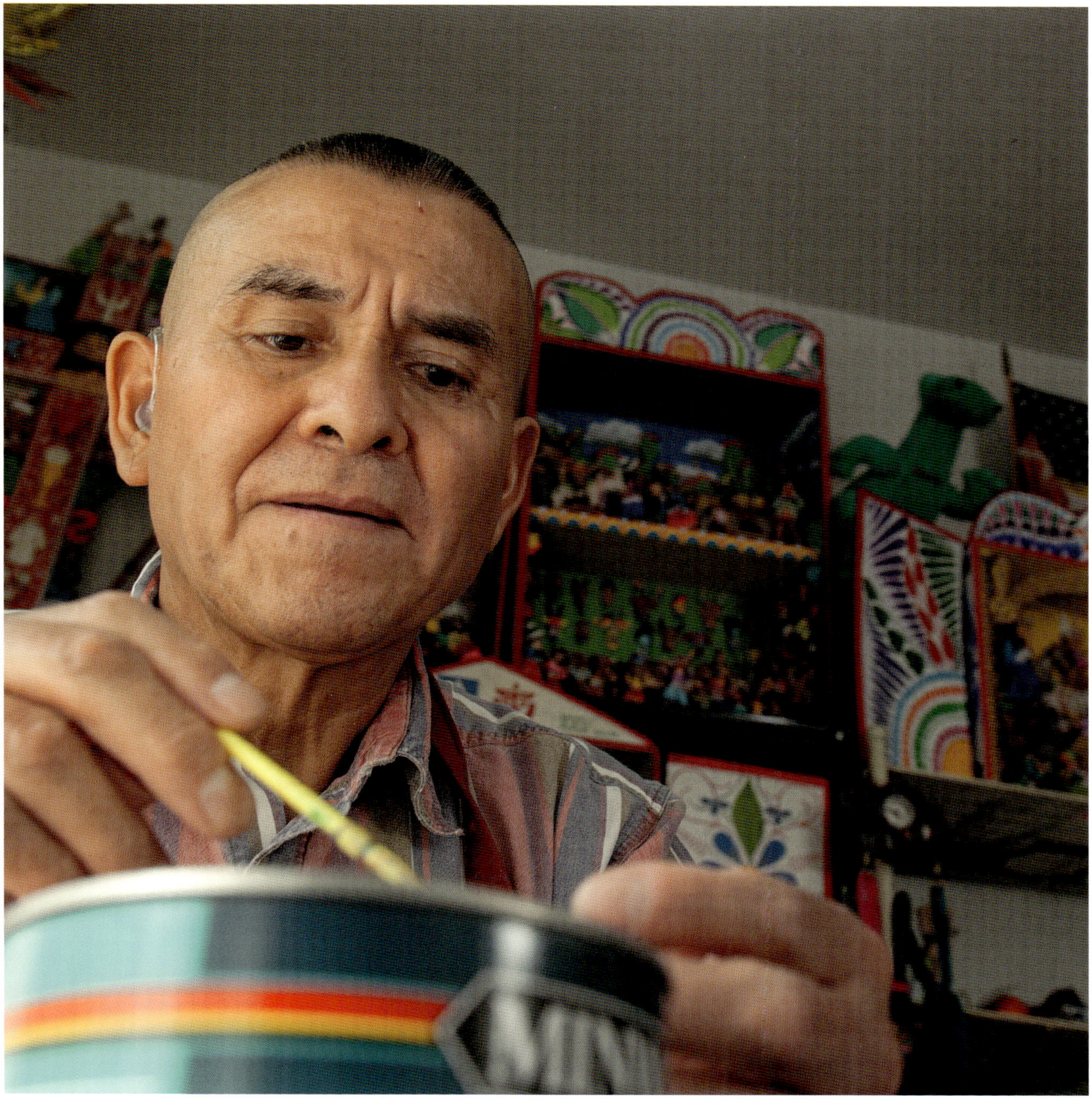

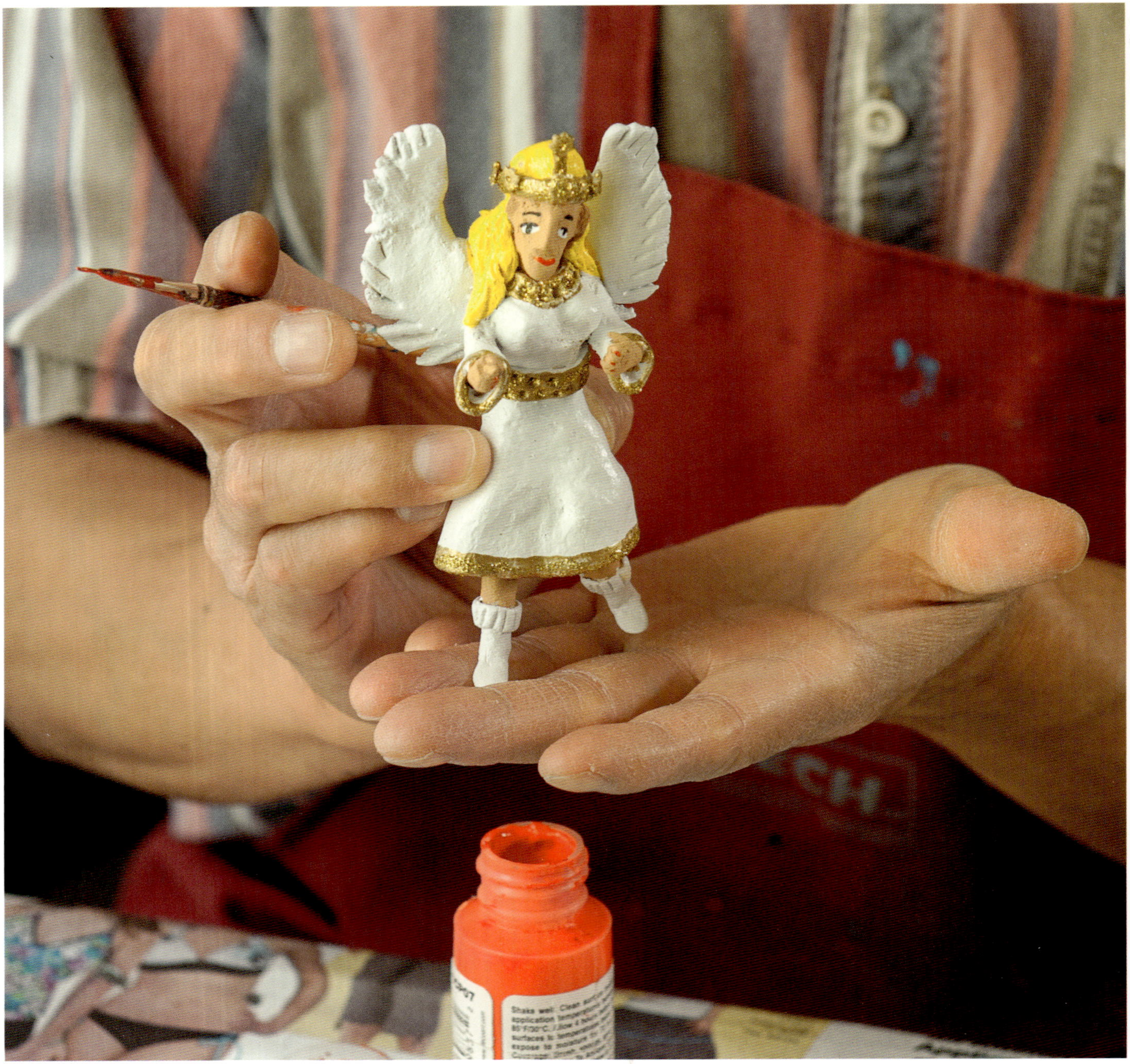

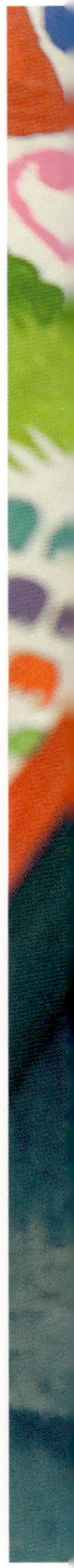

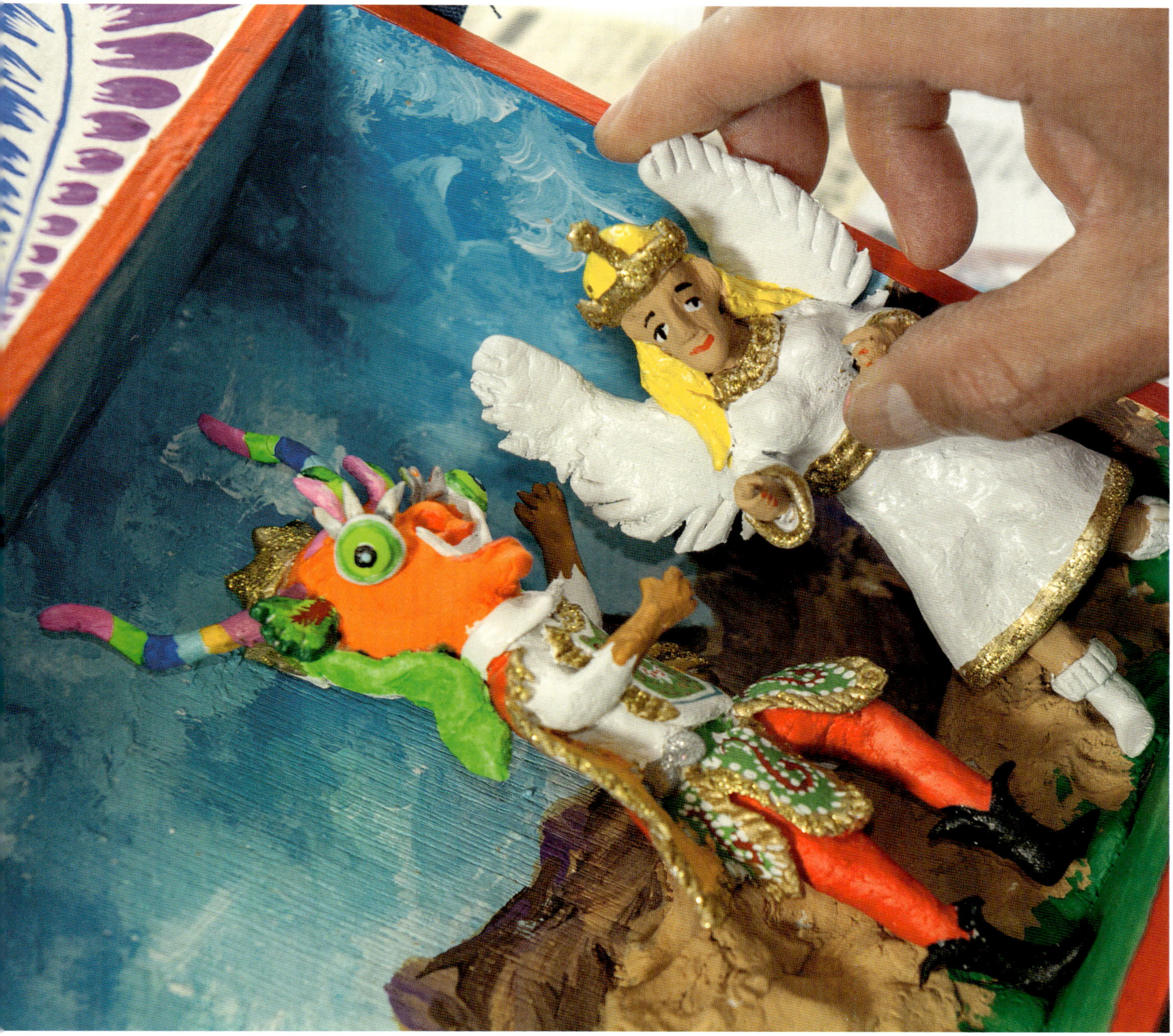

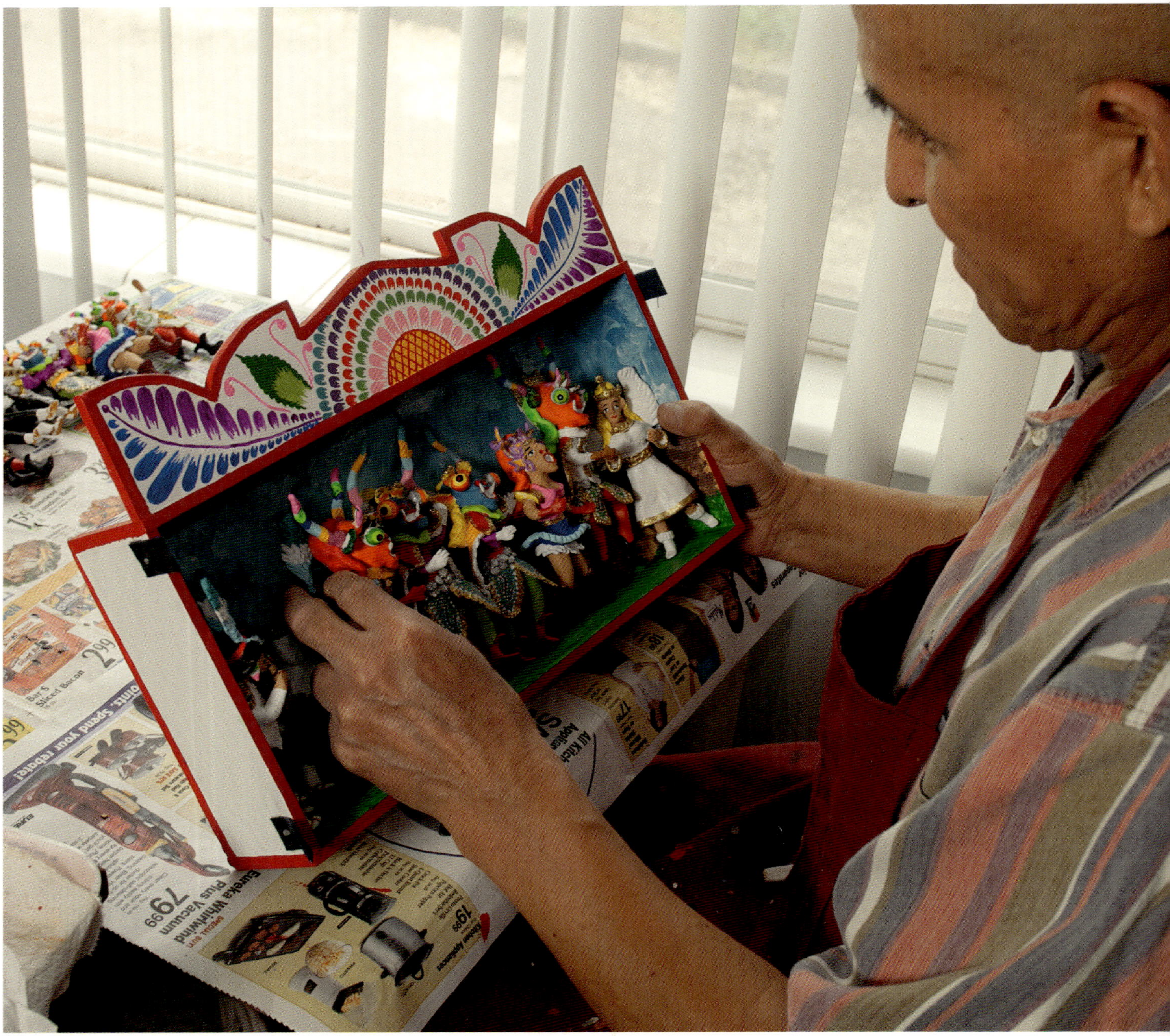

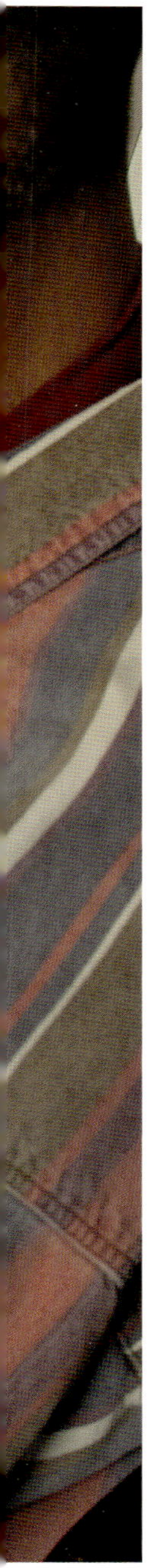

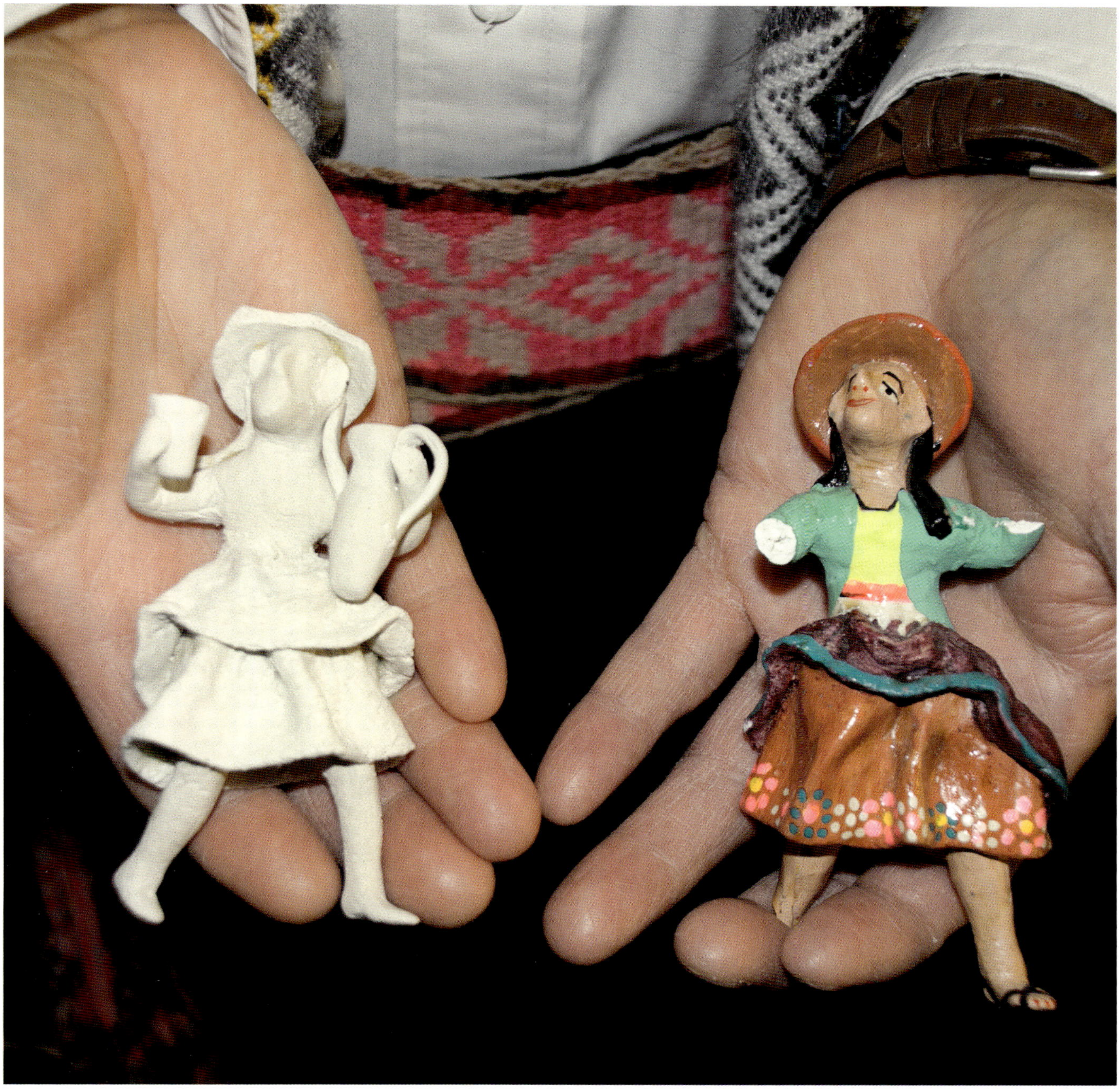

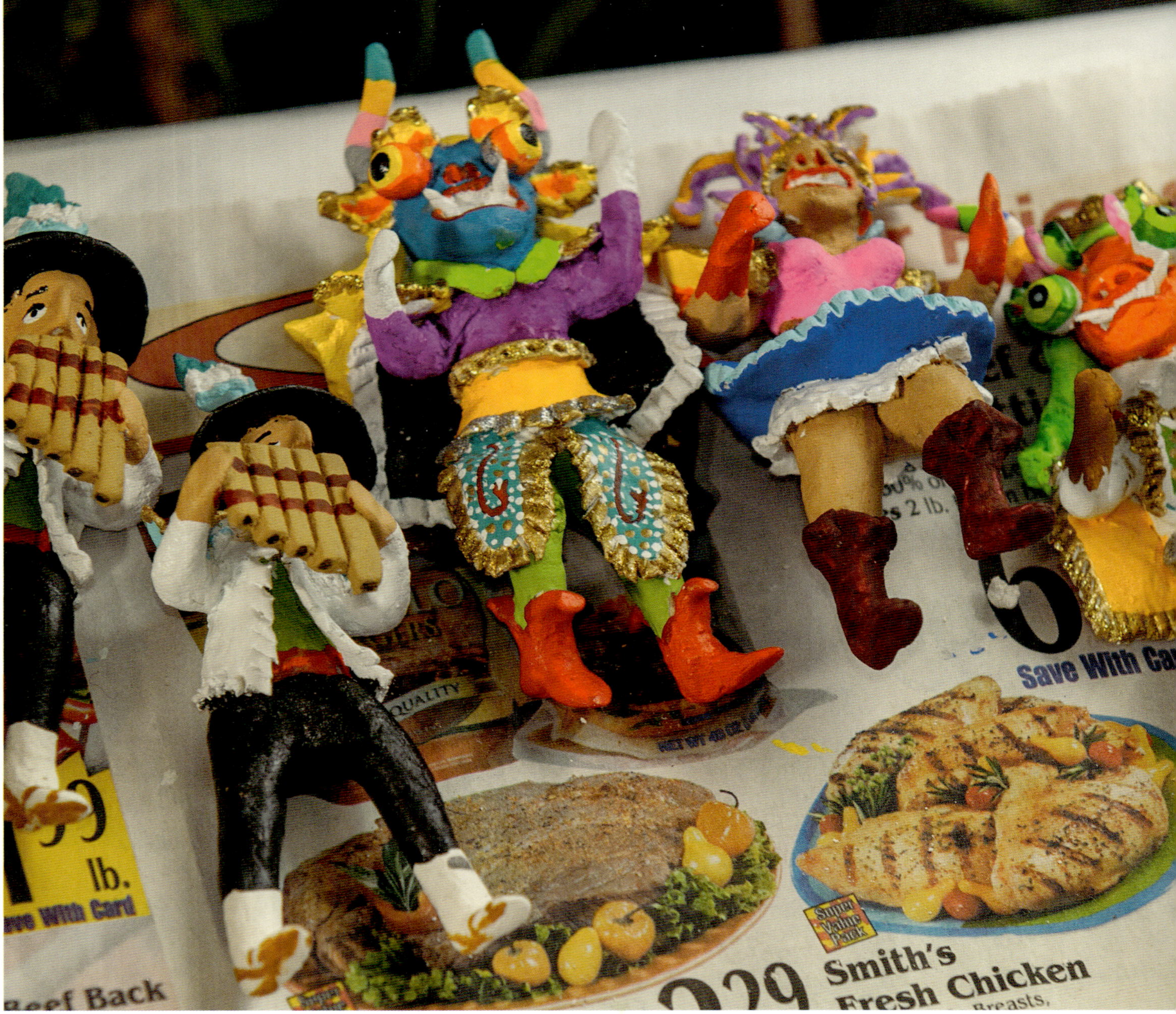
Smith's
Fresh Chicken

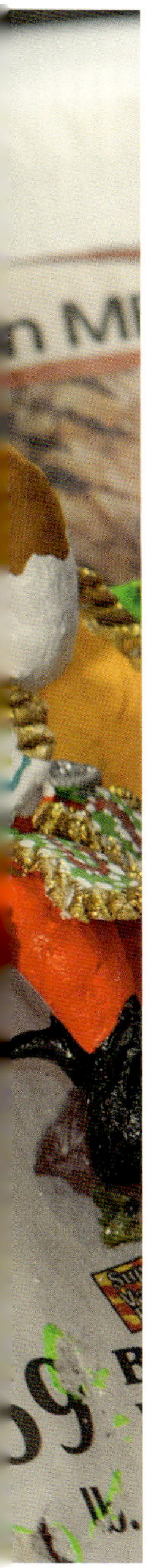

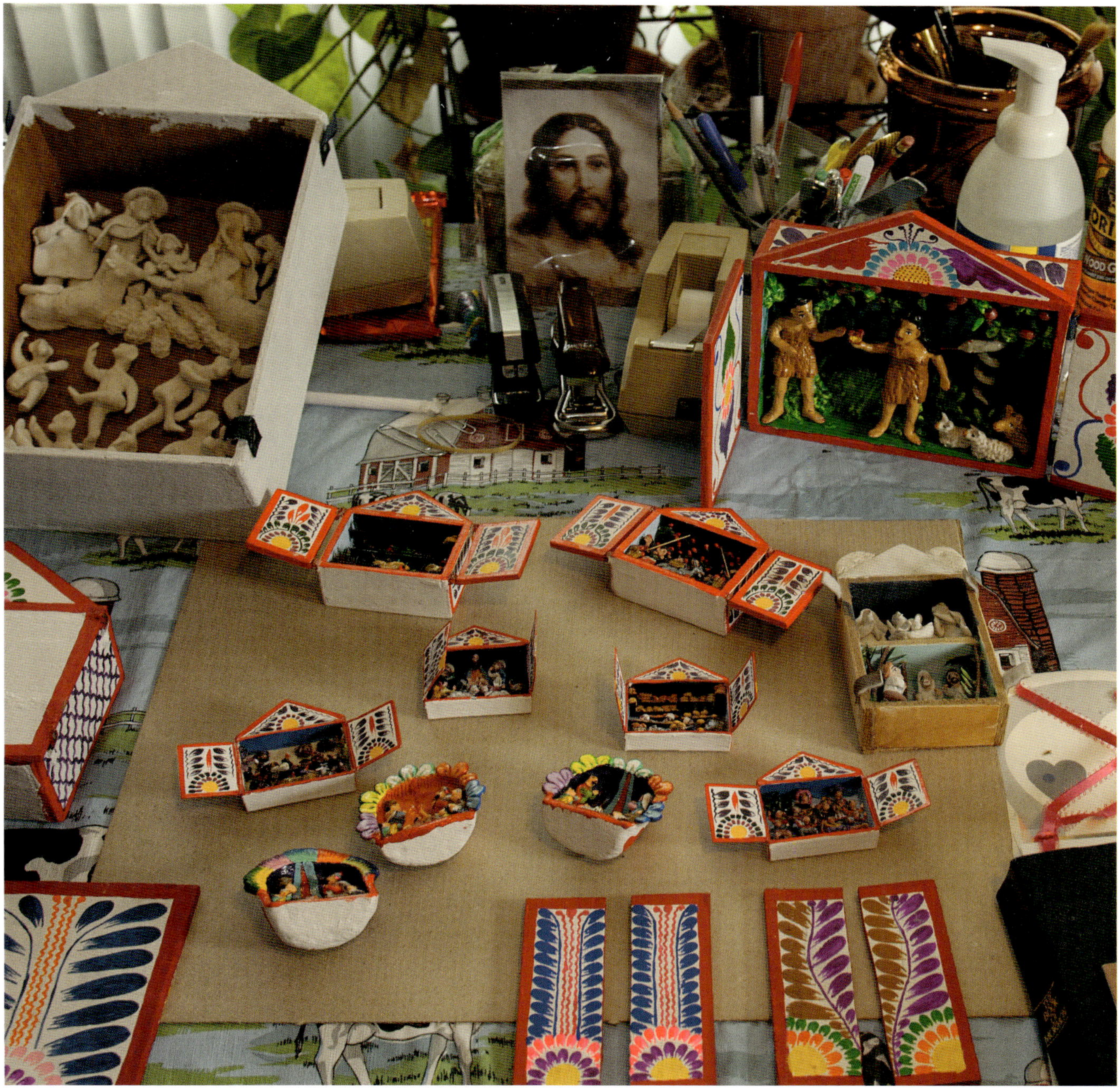

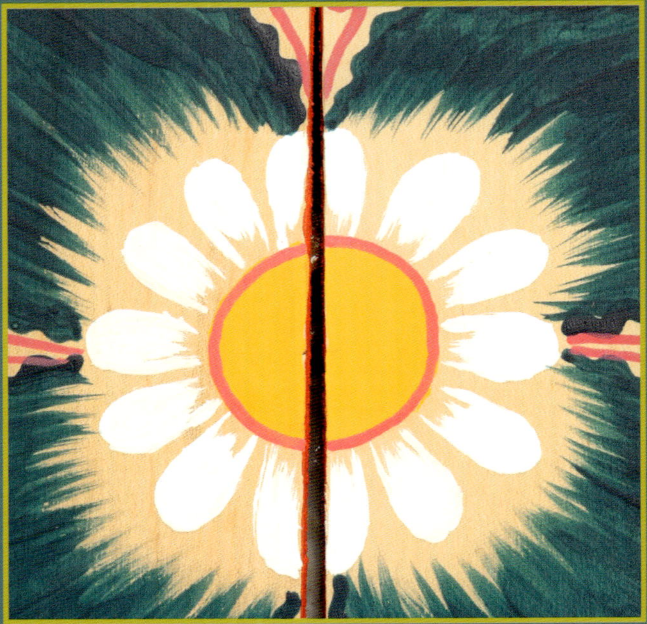
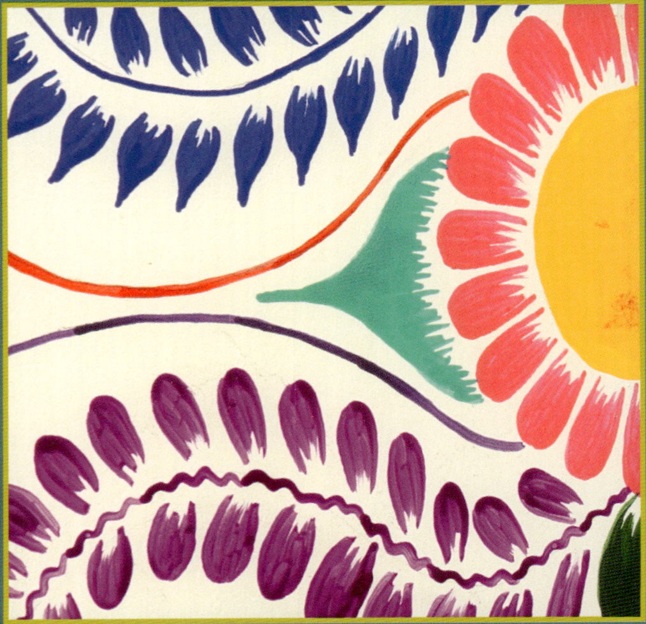
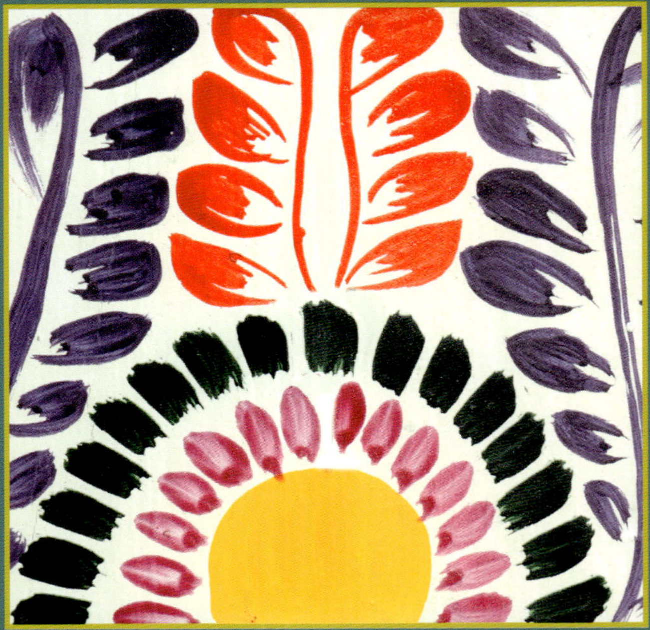
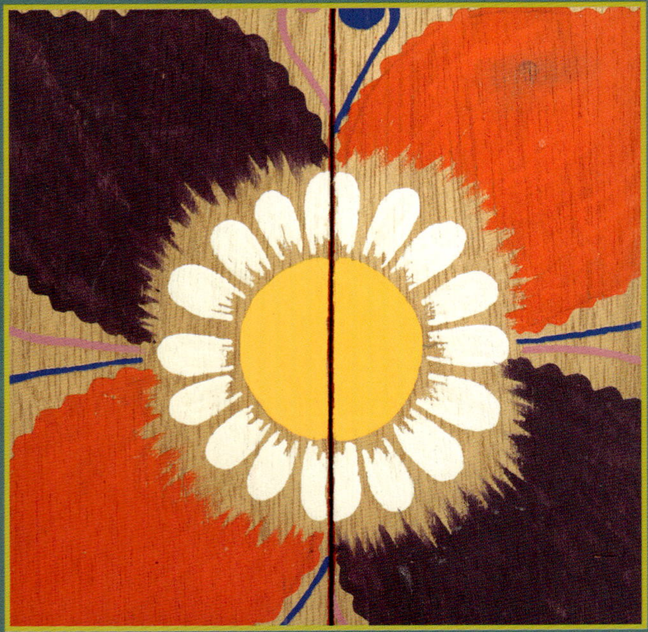

My Art

These are just small pieces that I might sell in craft stores for the average visitor, who maybe has a budget of under a hundred dollars to buy something. To display the retablos, I would combine traditional crafts of Peru, one of which was hand-painting large gourds. I would cut a hand-painted gourd in half to create an open book, with the interior of the hollow gourd filled with figures, combining two traditional Peruvian folk arts into a new form. Besides the large, gigantic gourds and boxes I made, I also innovated very small miniatures, placing retablos inside eggshells, or inside walnut shells that would open and close, or inside a little, tiny, single Chiclets Gum box, or a matchbox, or a pistachio shell.

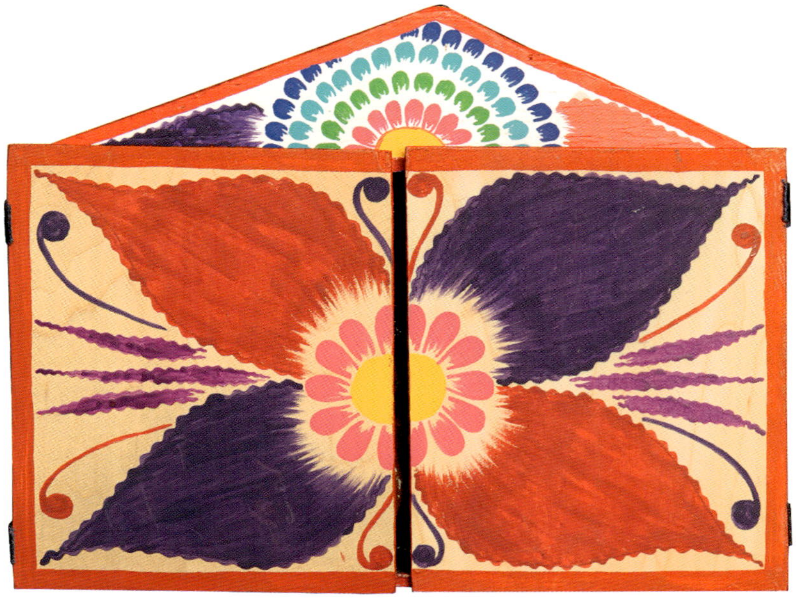

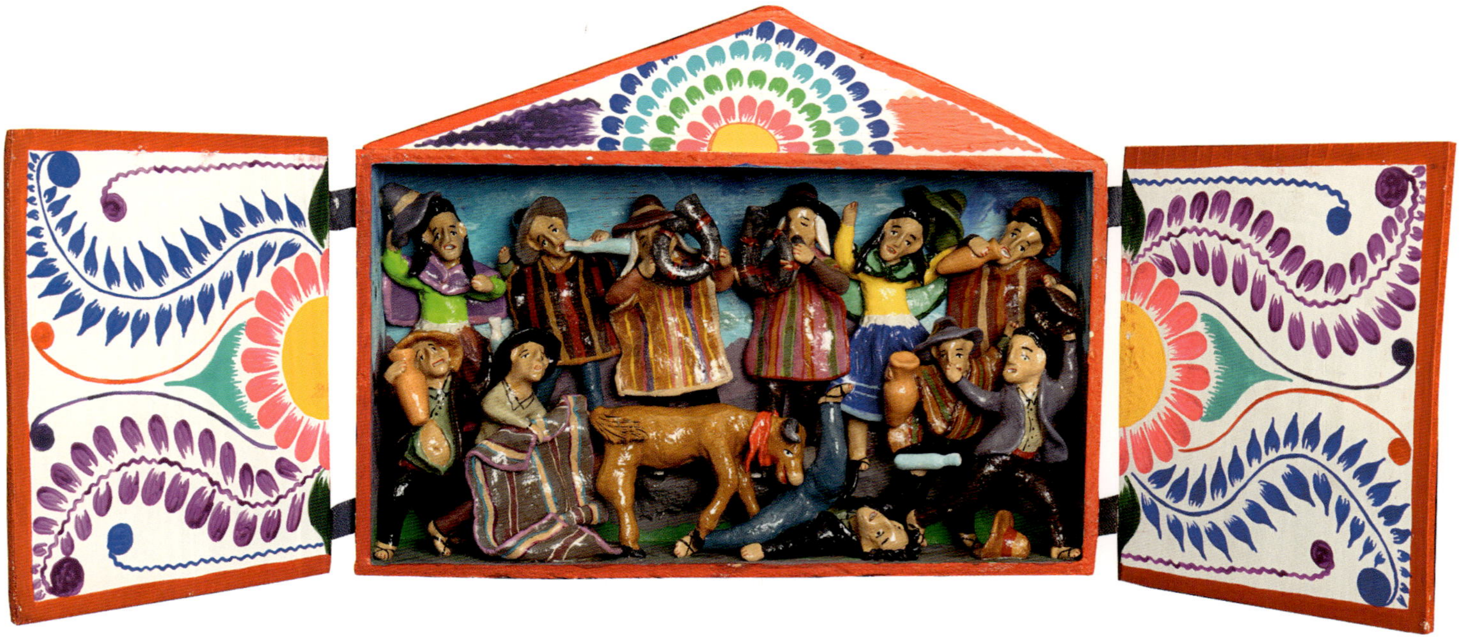

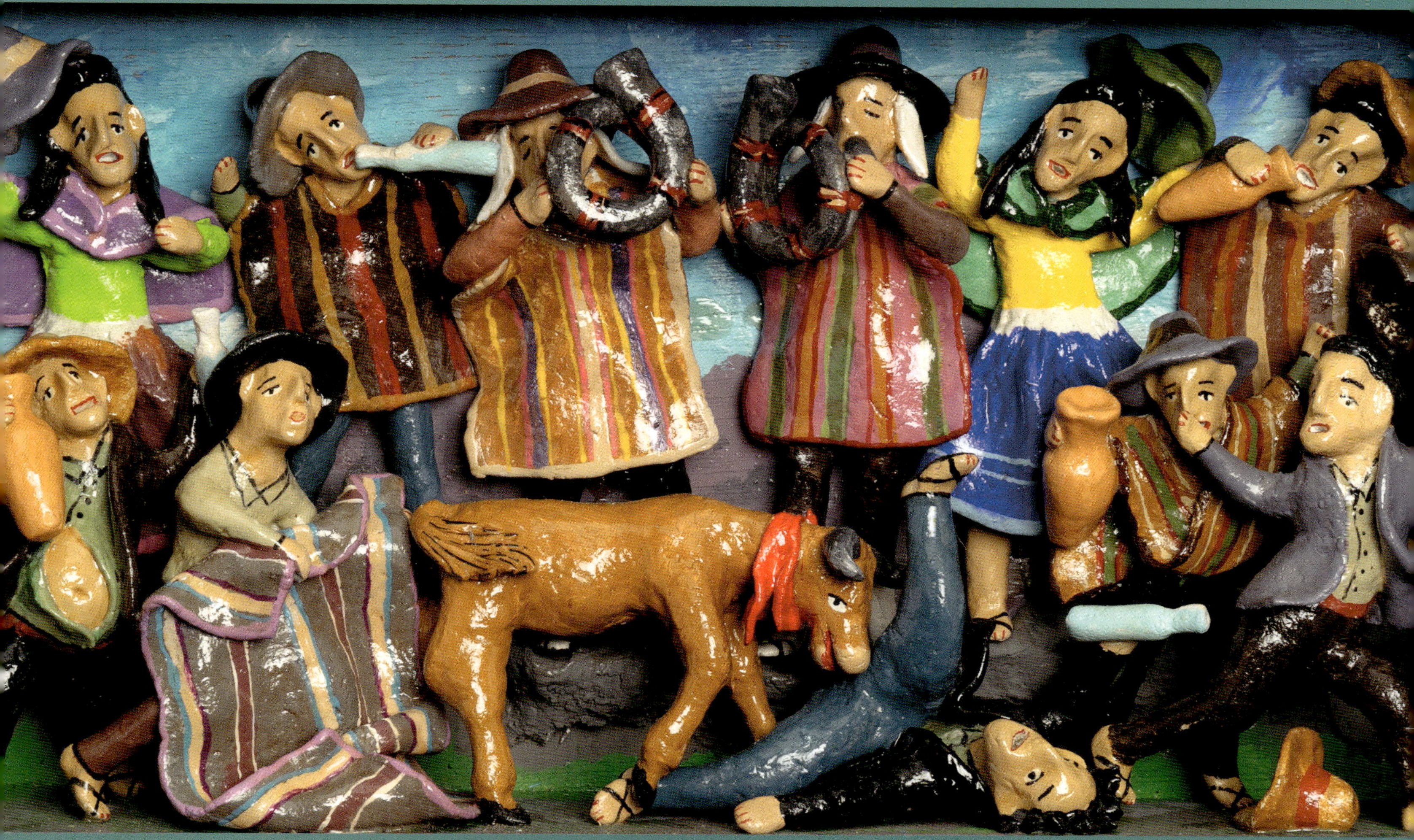

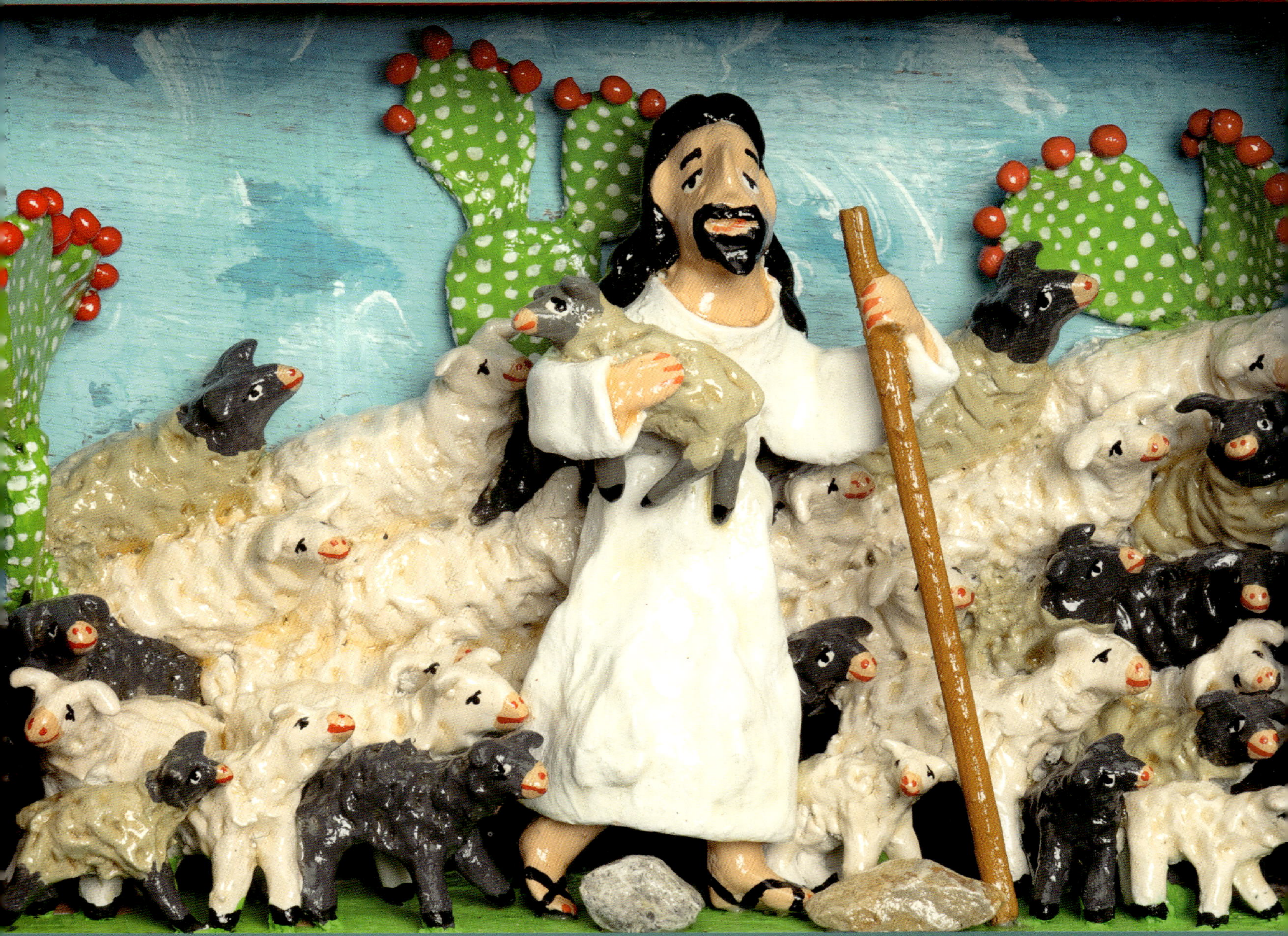

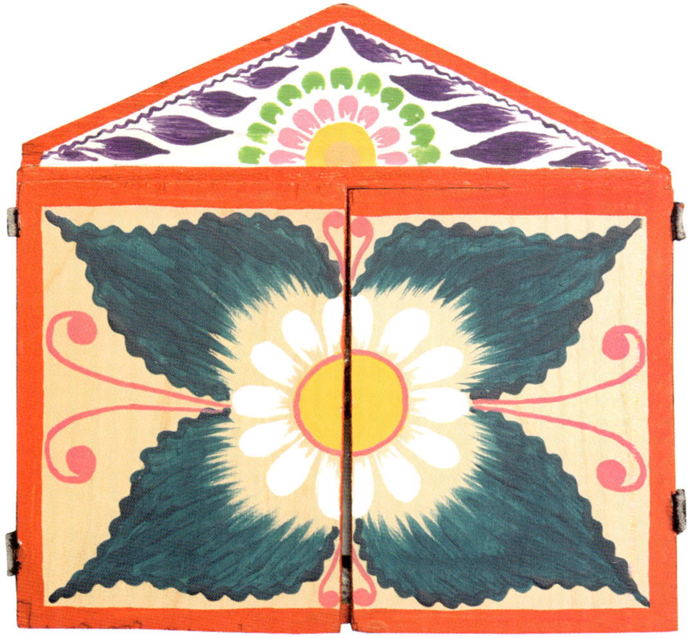

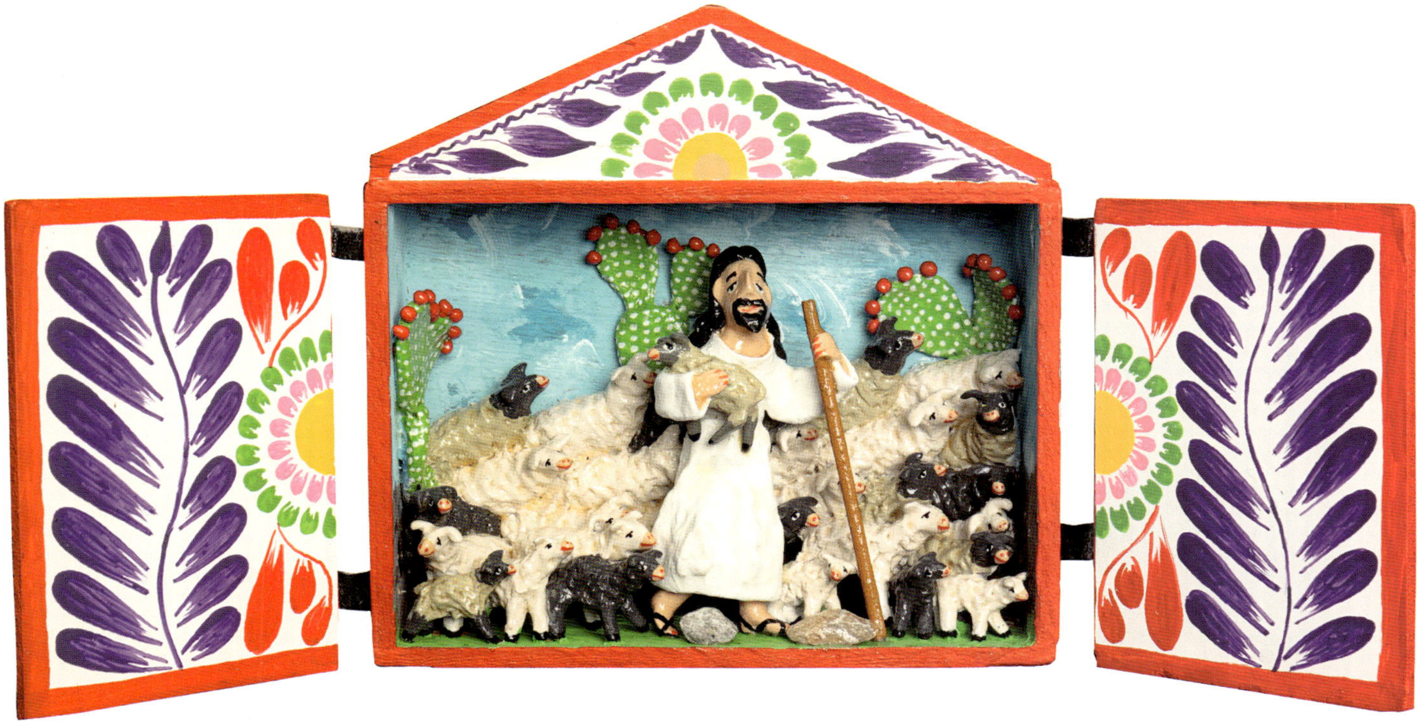

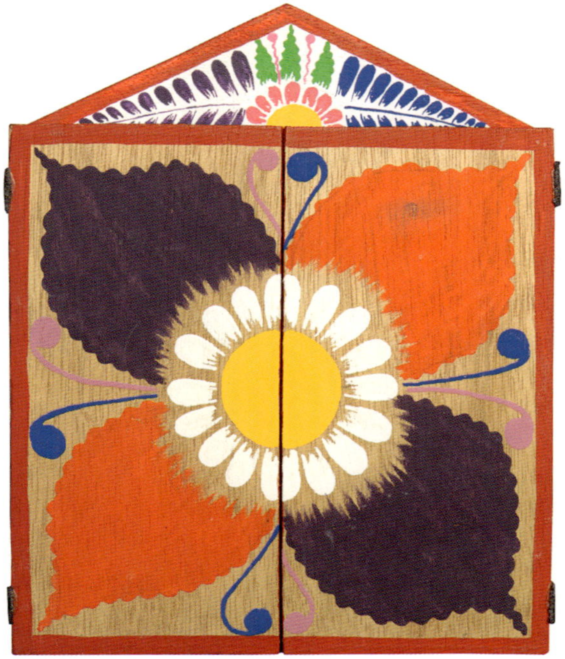

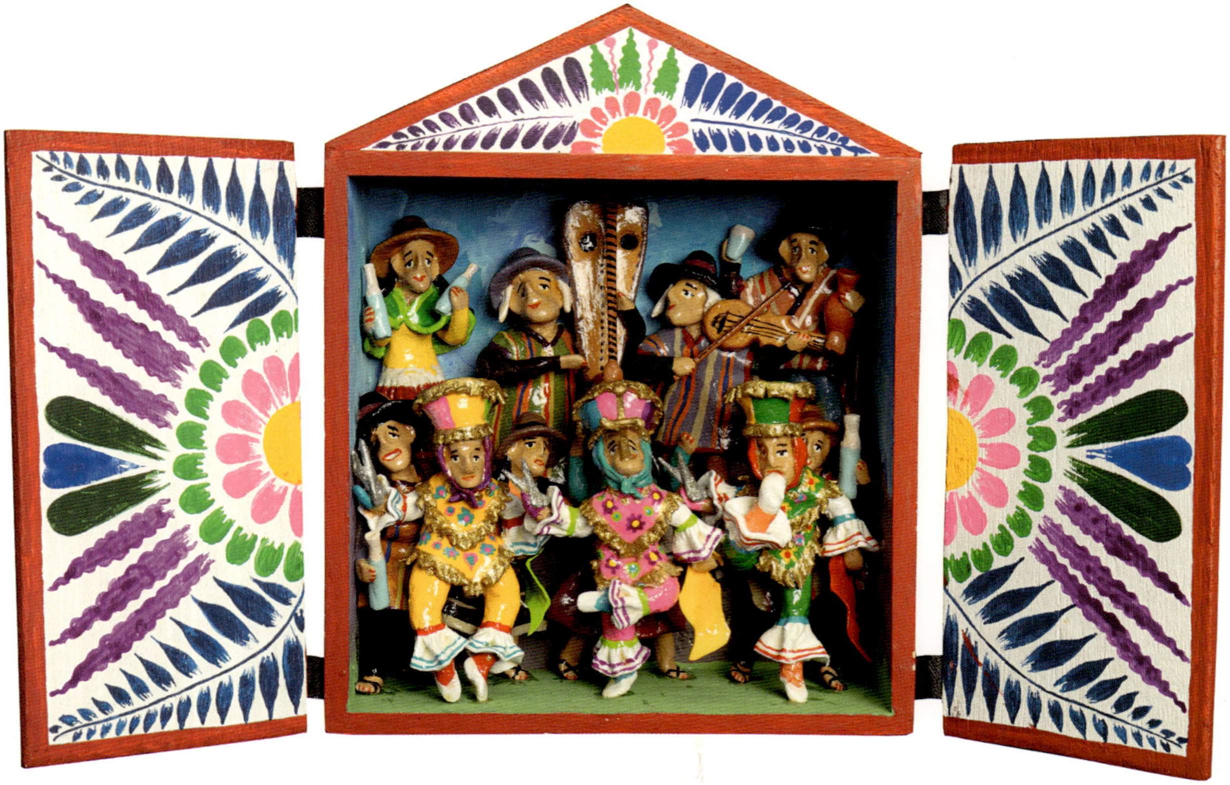

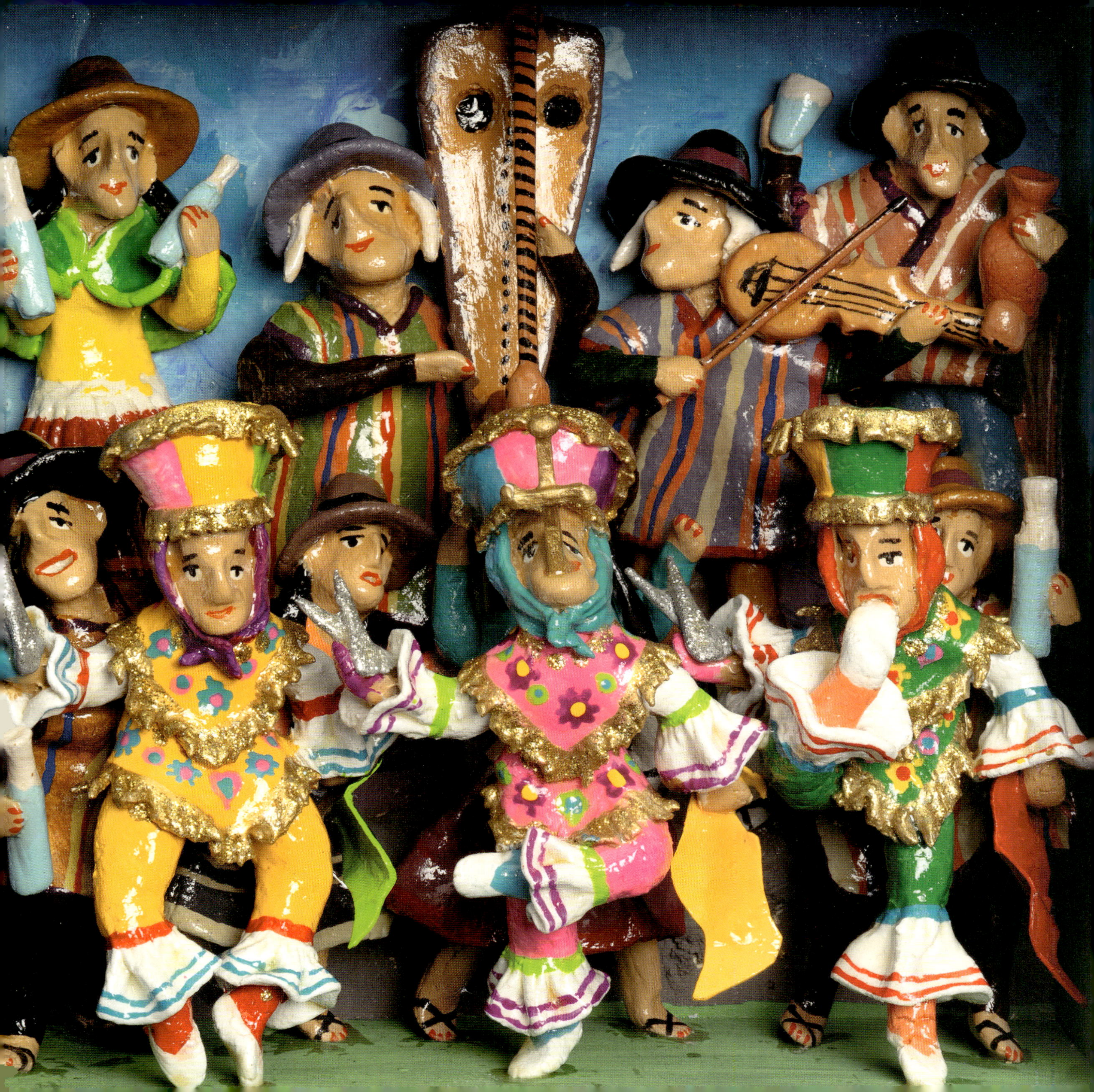

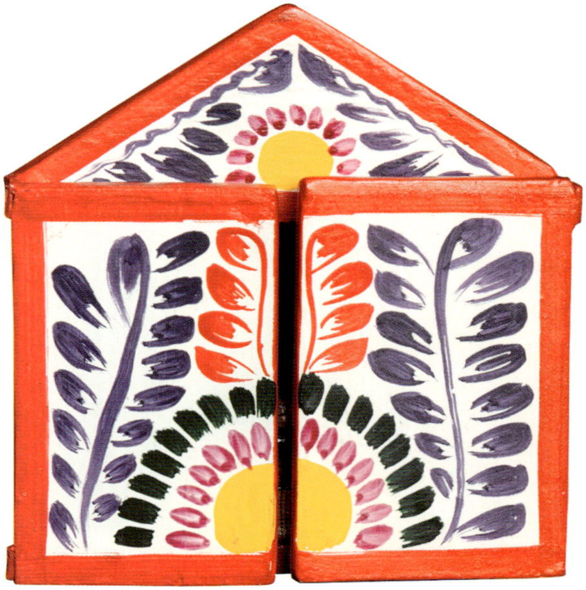

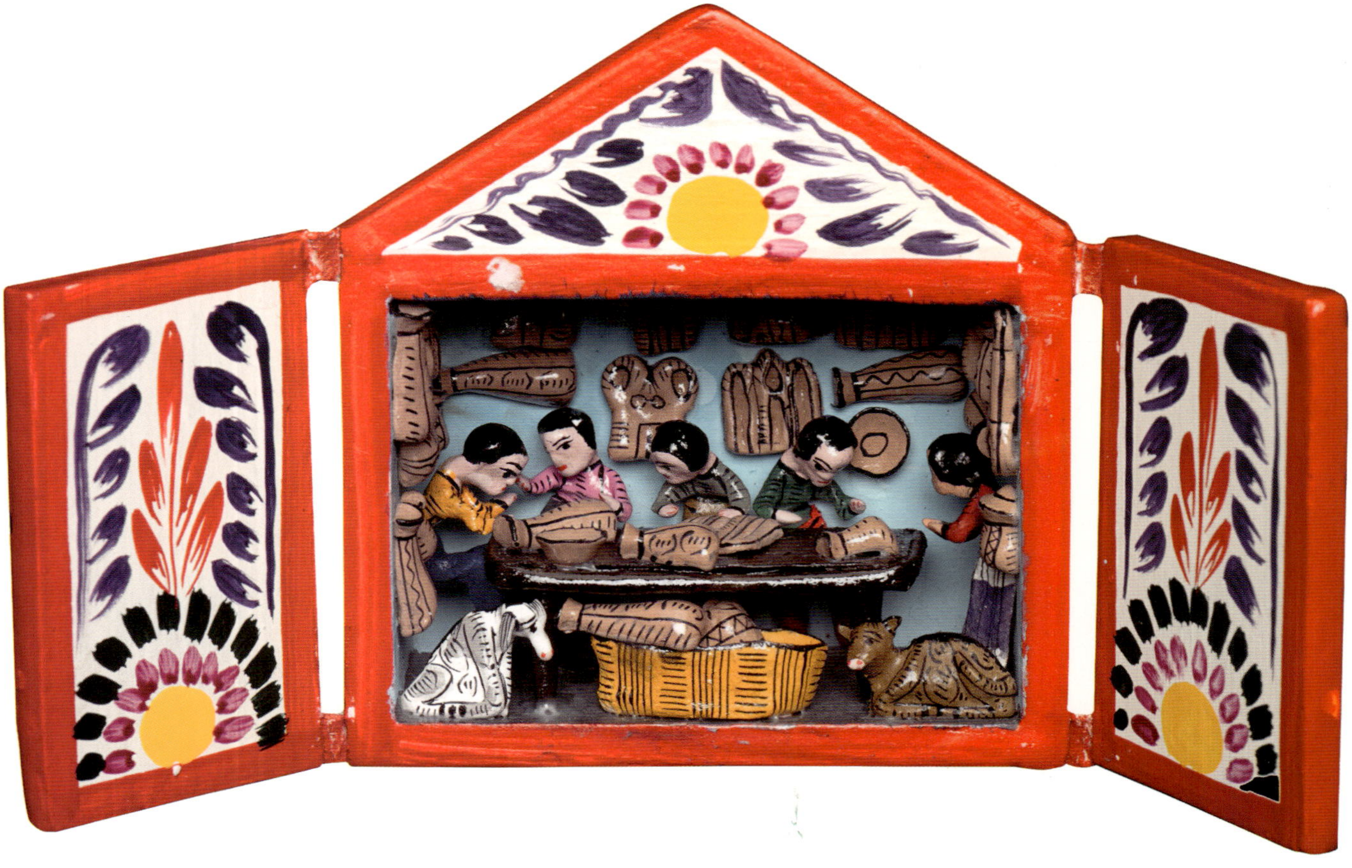

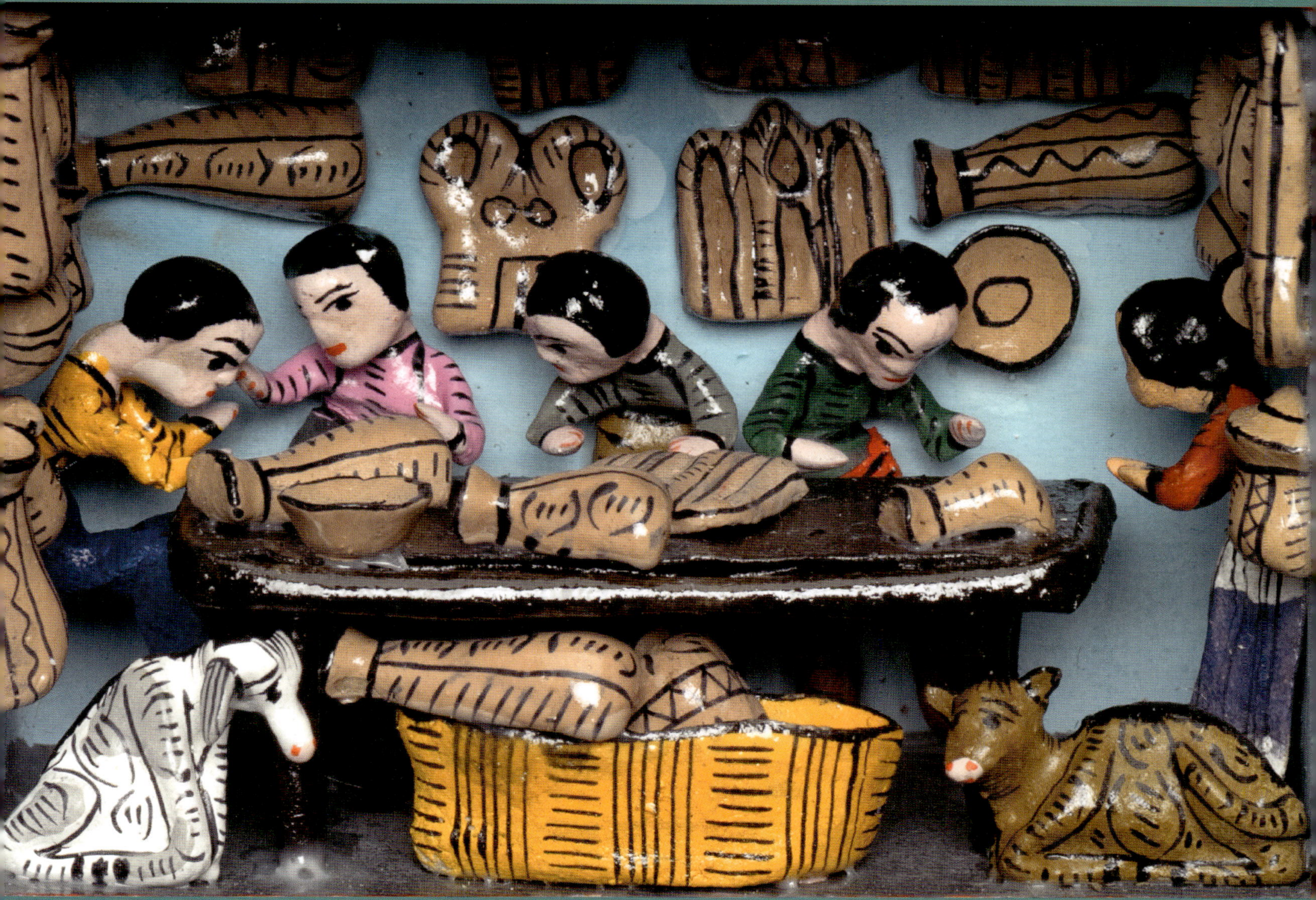

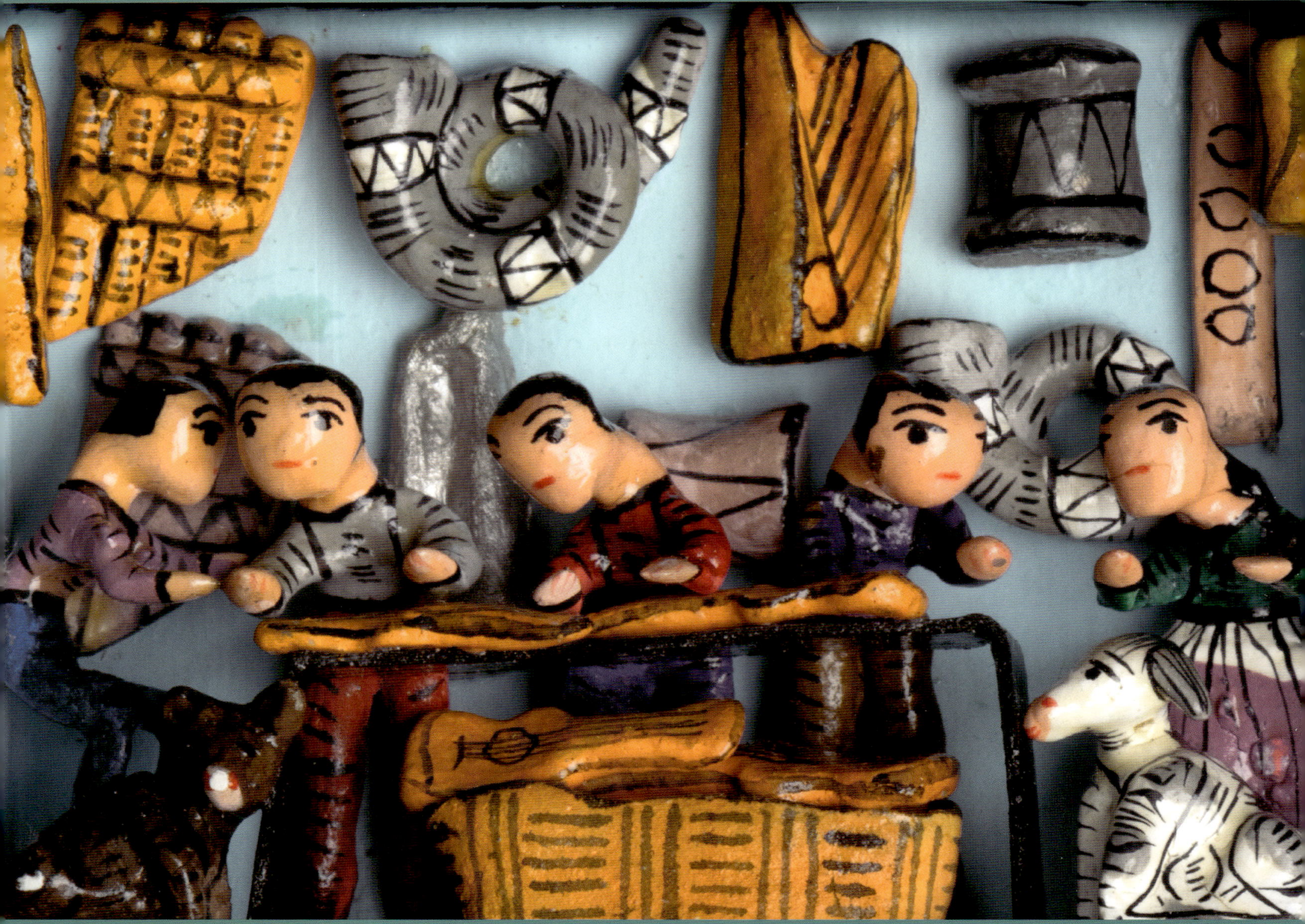

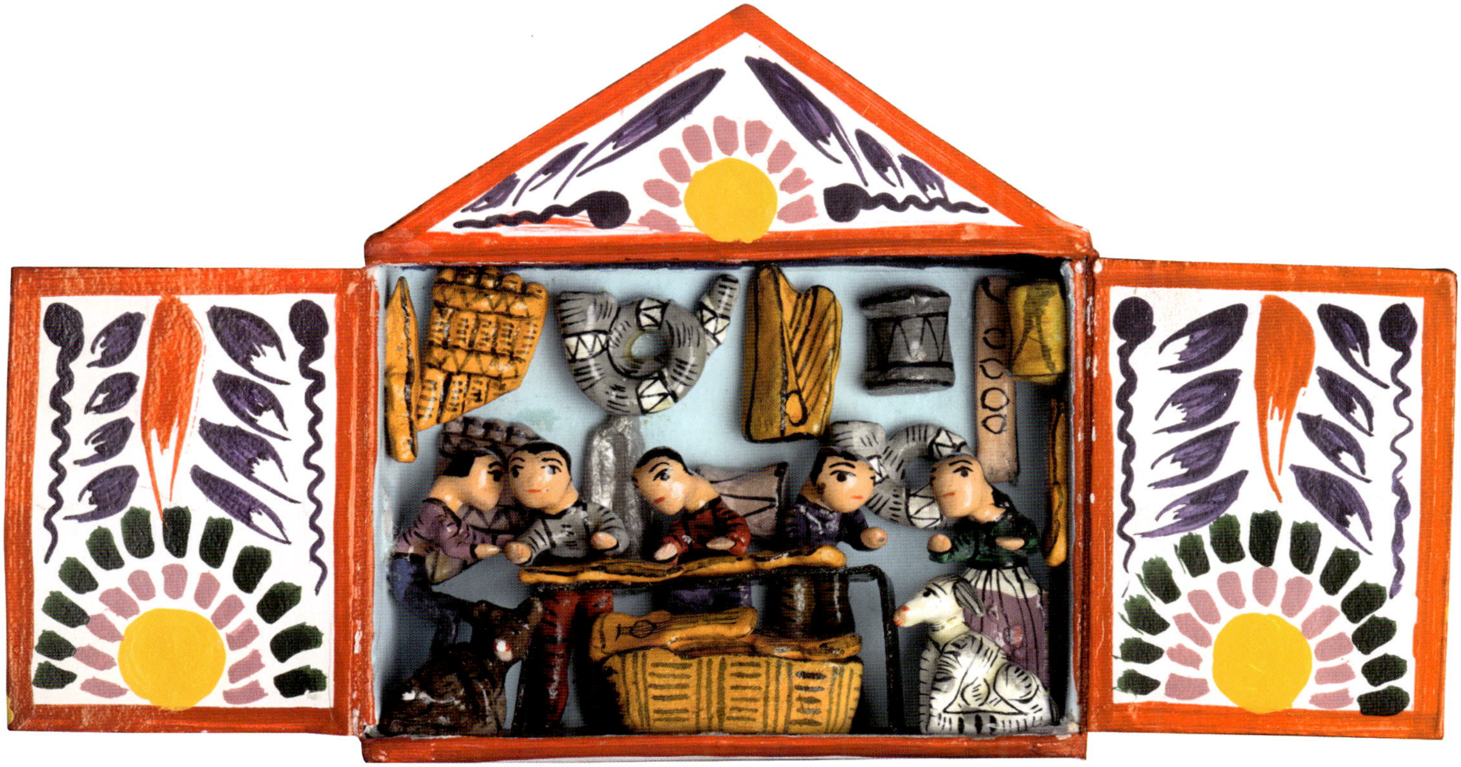

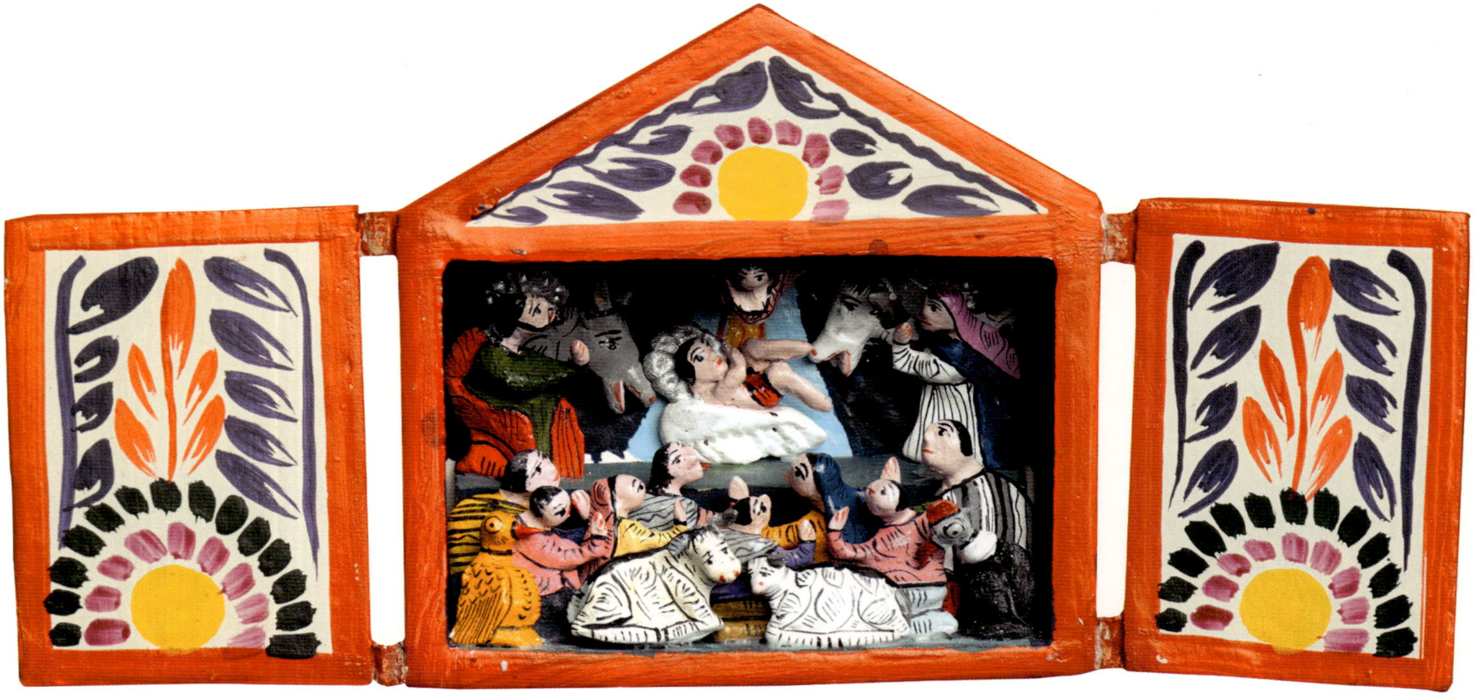

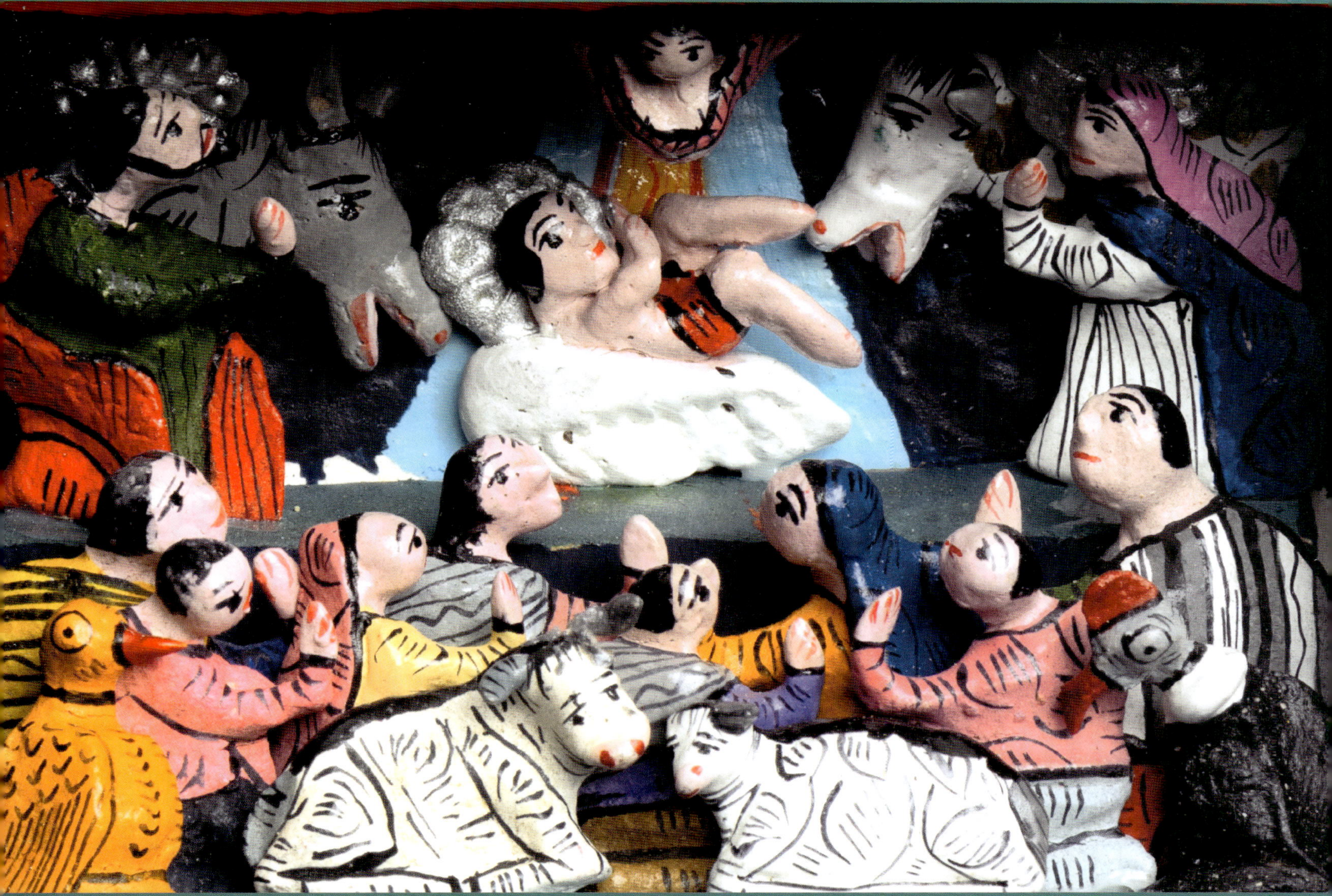

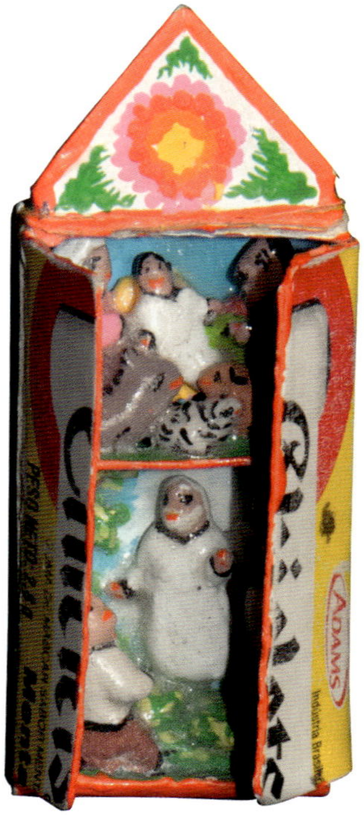

ADAMS

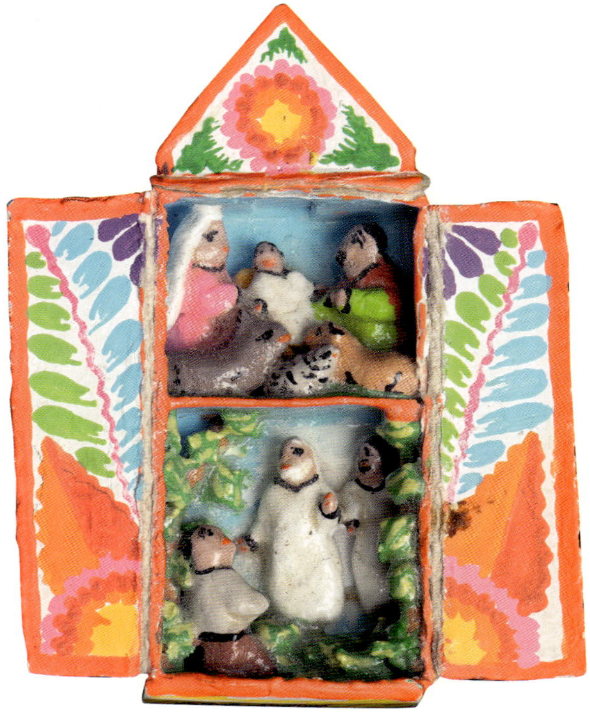

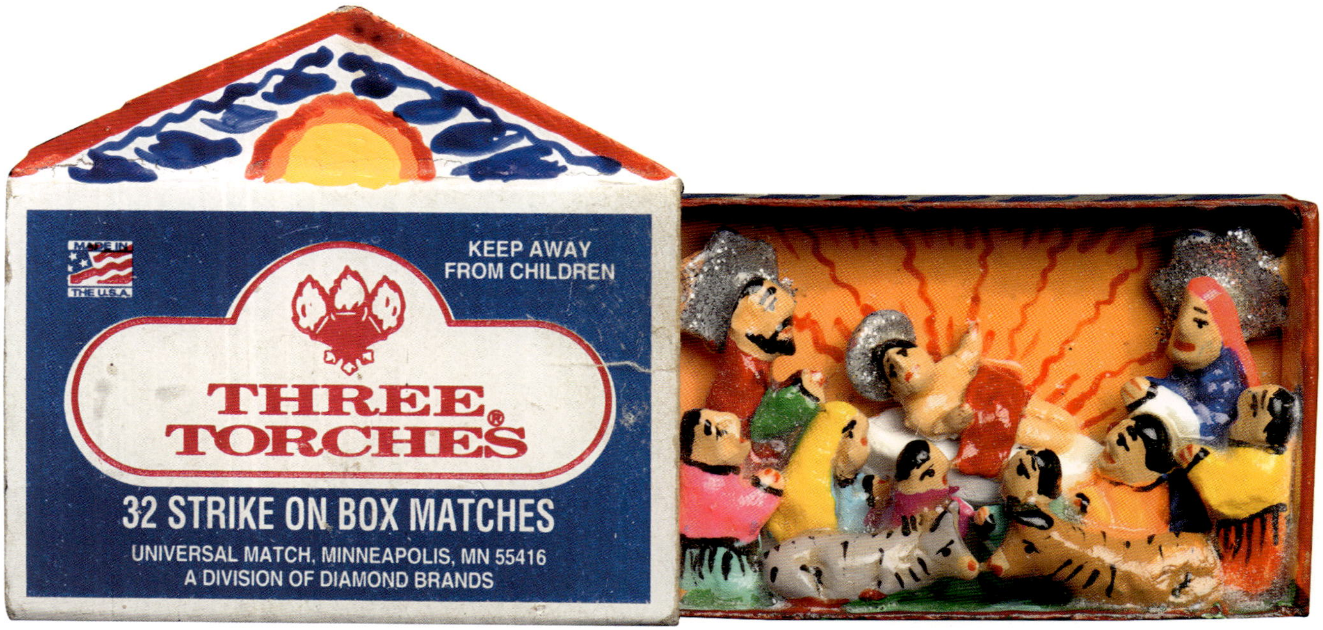

MADE IN
THE U.S.A.
KEEP AWAY
FROM CHILDREN
THREE
TORCHES®
32 STRIKE ON BOX MATCHES
UNIVERSAL MATCH, MINNEAPOLIS, MN 55416
A DIVISION OF DIAMOND BRANDS

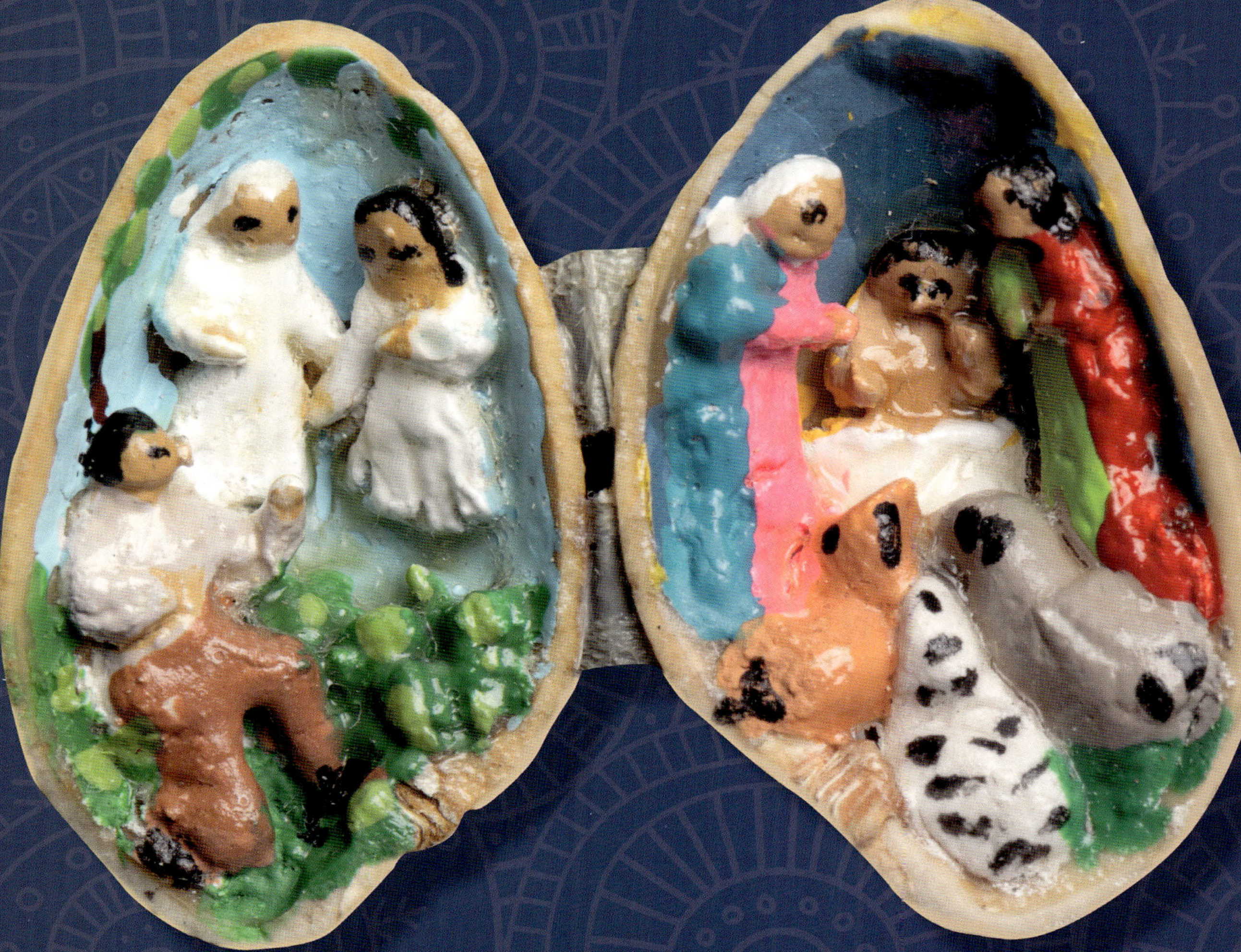

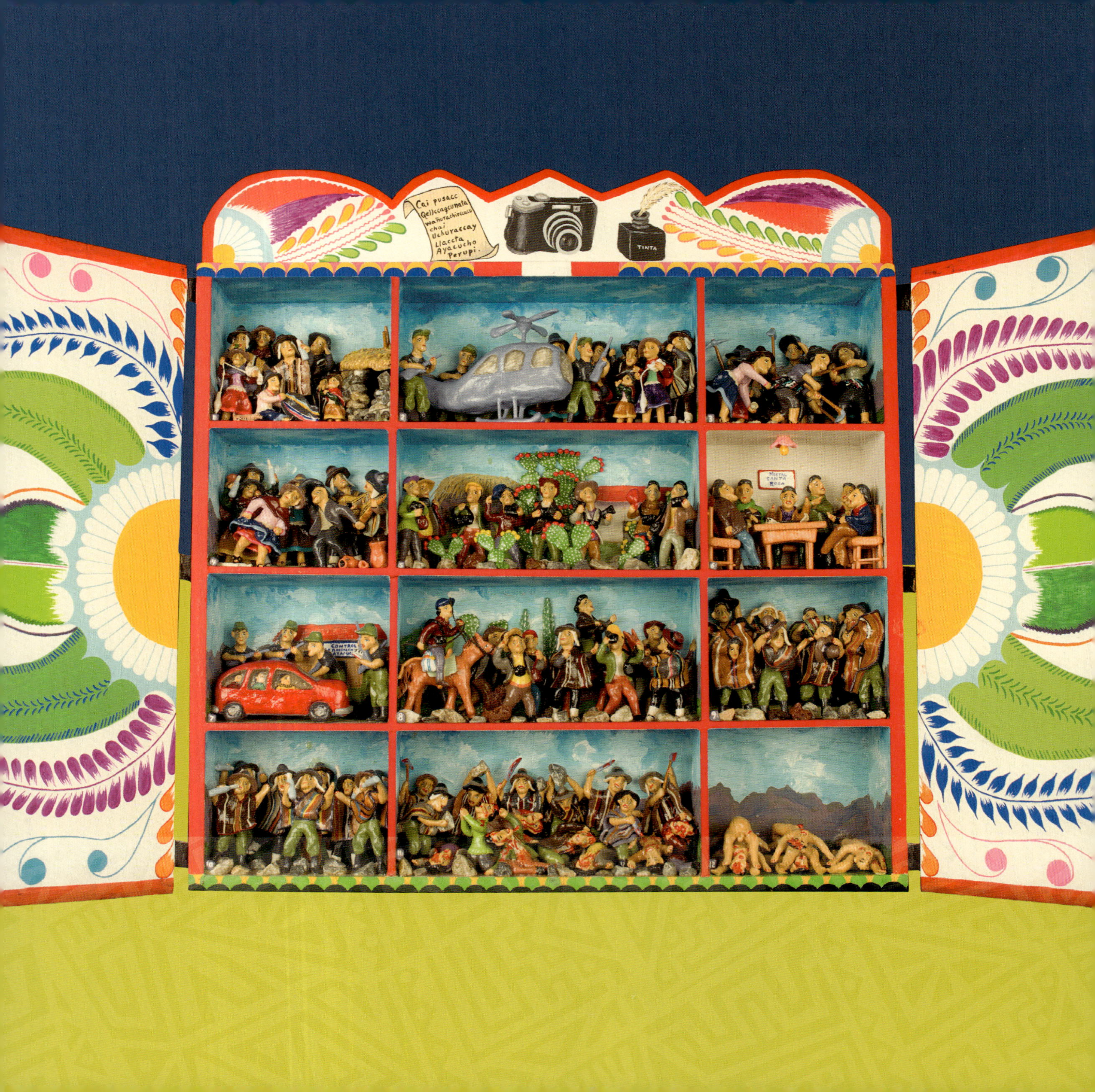
Cai pusacc Qellccaqcunata wañurachircacc chai Uchuraccay Llaccta Ayacucho Perupi.
TINTA

The Tragedy in Uchuraccay

The Killing of Eight Peruvian Journalists

In 1983, eight journalists were murdered in Uchuraccay, a village in the Peruvian province of Huanta, Ayacucho Region. Although it seemed that the guilty parties of this terrible episode would never be identified, I decided to make my own inquiry concerning the death of my friend and fellow student Octavio Infante García, one of the eight journalist martyrs. To do this safely, I thought it would be best to mix with the local population, dressed in their traditional clothing and assuming the character of a commoner. I rode a burro from the city of Huamanga, Ayacucho, to Uchuraccay, where the reporters had met their death, and then to the home of my friend in the small mountain village of Sachabamba.

After traveling through the various places where the journalists had gone, I made a retablo to visually record the truthful history. It is not a fantasy but a faithful version of the events as told to me by the helpful mountain people in the original language of the native Inca Empire, Quechua. I made it as a fitting tribute to all the brave journalists killed around the world.

This retablo, *The Tragedy in Uchuraccay,* has twelve interior compartments, numbered and titled. Each tells a distinct part of the story.

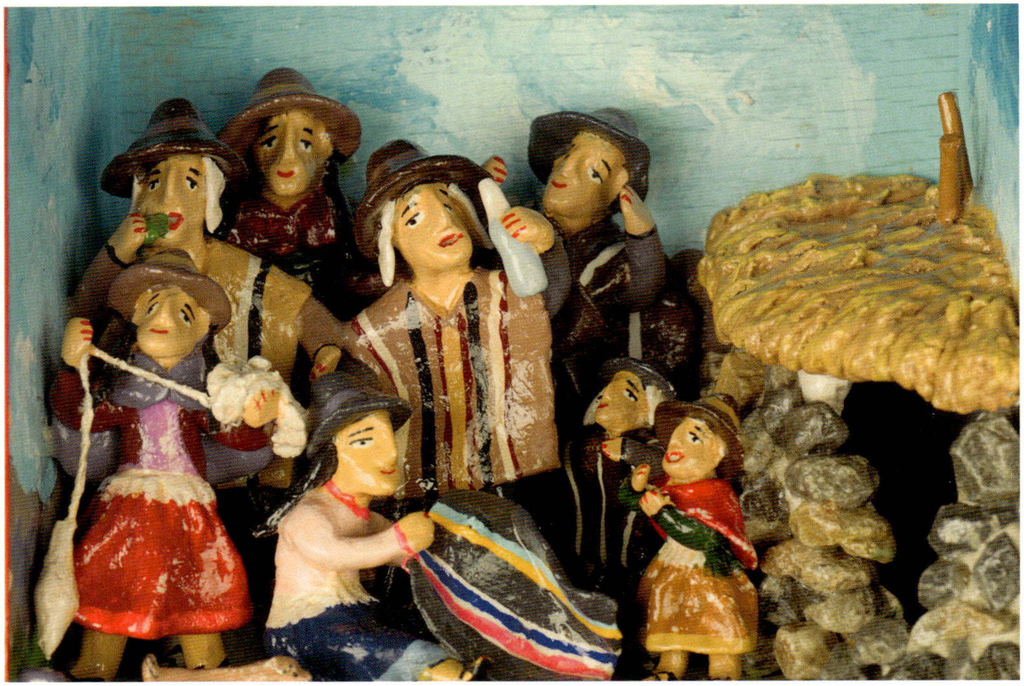

1. THE UCHURACCAYNOS: They are humble people who live in inhospitable places of the Andes, much the same as they have for over five hundred years. They speak the Quechua language and are generally illiterate in Spanish. Their homes are small huts built with stacked stone walls and simple thatched roofs. In the main square, only a few huts are raised; the rest are scattered over great distances along the slopes of the hills. They are very friendly and hospitable to outsiders, although they have limited contact with modern civilization.

They live from what they produce from the land and the pasture animals they tend. They make their own traditional clothing by spinning wool yarn from llamas, alpacas, guanacos, and sheep, then weaving or knitting it into ponchos, blankets, socks, pants, skirts, blouses, belts, hats, scarves, etc. They make sandals from the hides of llamas and bulls. They make ropes from leather or wool, each for different uses. The weather is variable; it rains from time to time and sometimes is cold and damp, and other times warm and sunny. They have great respect for the dead.

2. HELICOPTER and COMMONERS: When the villagers of Uchuraccay saw this flying metal machine, many were surprised and somewhat scared. They associated the surprise appearance of a helicopter with the dragonfly and this creature's ability to fly fast and hover in the air. The common people in the high plains of the Andes call dragonflies "cachi cachi" and associate their presence with a positive sign that someone is coming and will arrive soon.

As more people gathered, the arrival of the helicopter grew to be seen as a fortuitous messenger that visitors were coming. Through an interpreter, the soldiers promised to give the people every need and explained to them that they had come to warn them: "Those who come from above are your friends, and those who come on the roadway are your enemies." They then encouraged them to "defend yourself and kill them."

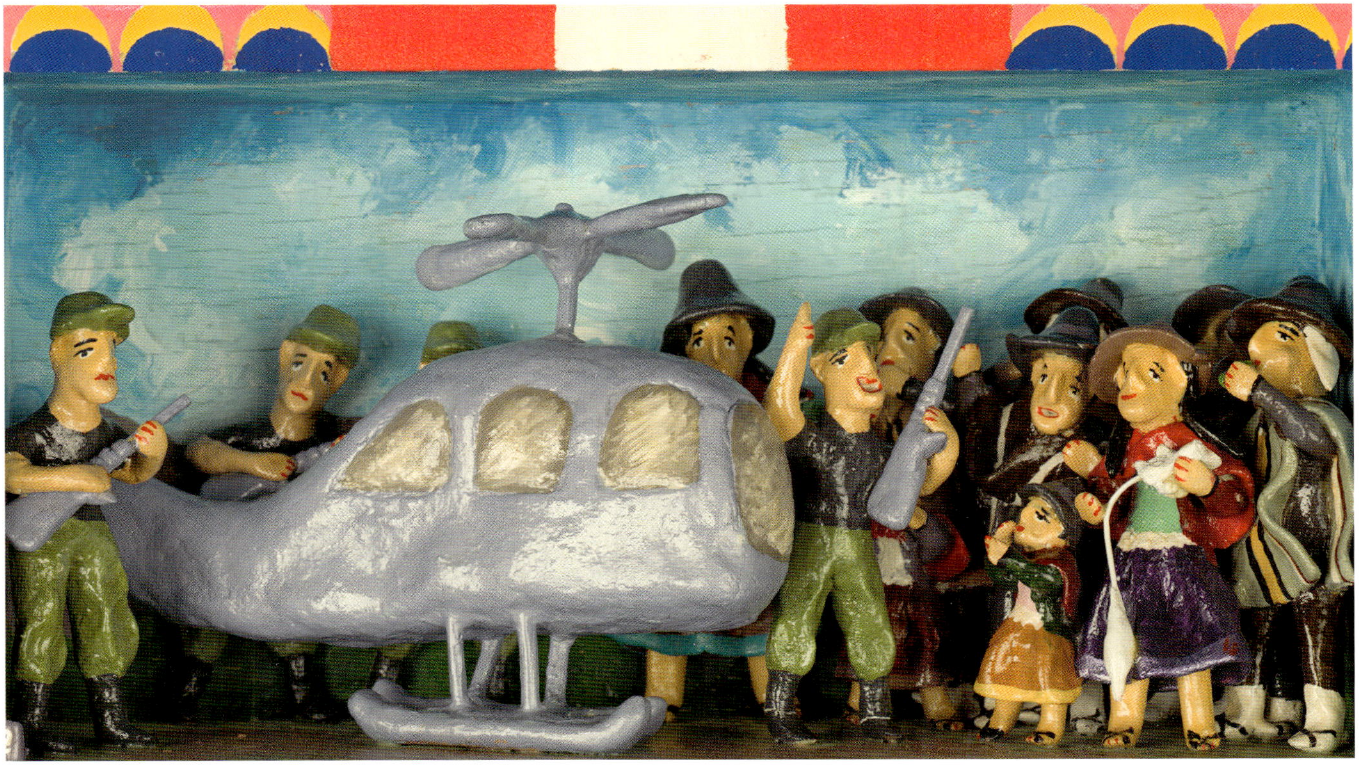

3. SOWING: The commoners are excellent workers of the land and grow a variety of potatoes and other tubers, root vegetables, and beans. Their principal meal is a dried potato soup combined with natural aromatic herbs. They also make cheese and dry jerky naturally in the sun or smoked over a fire.

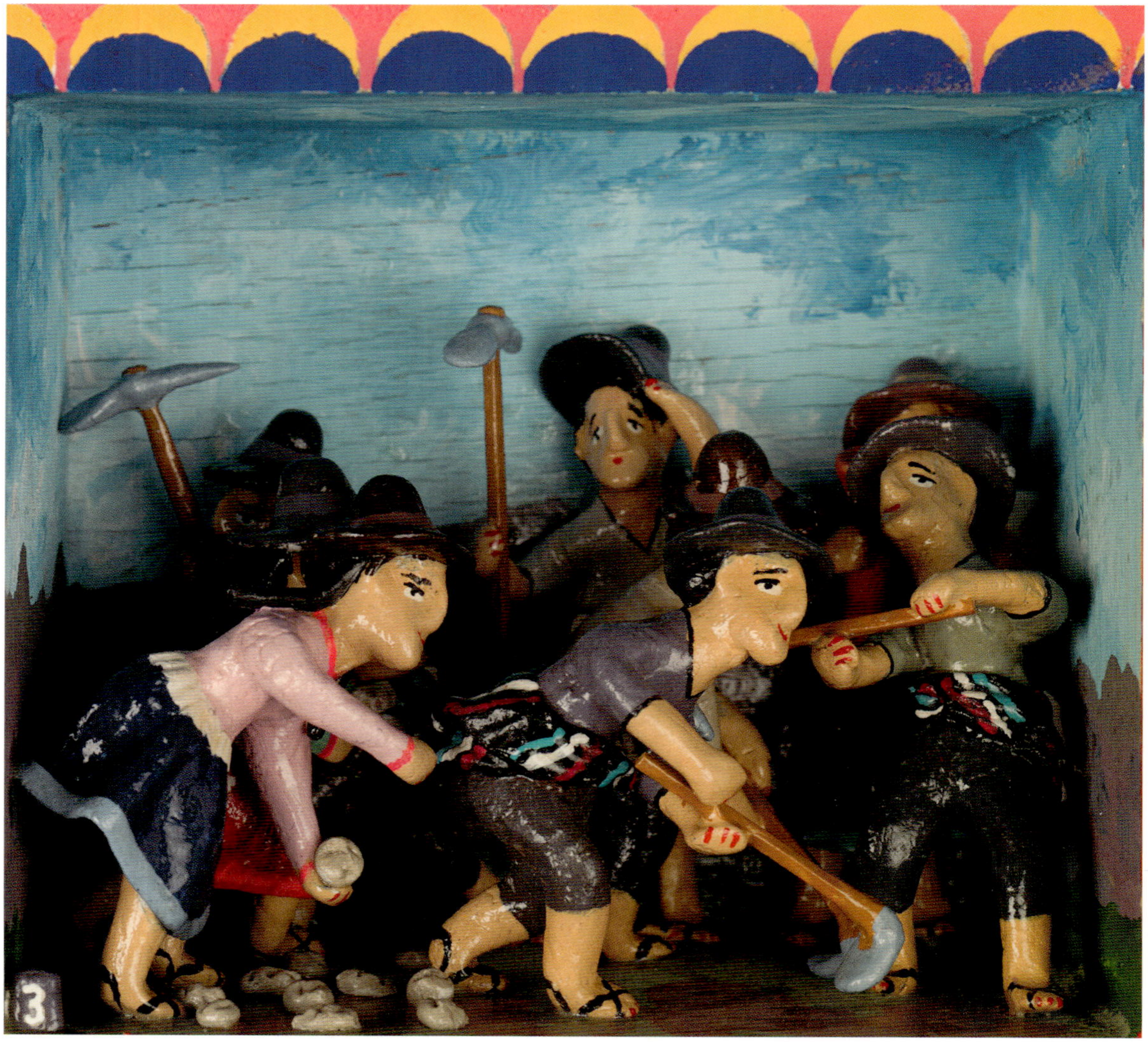

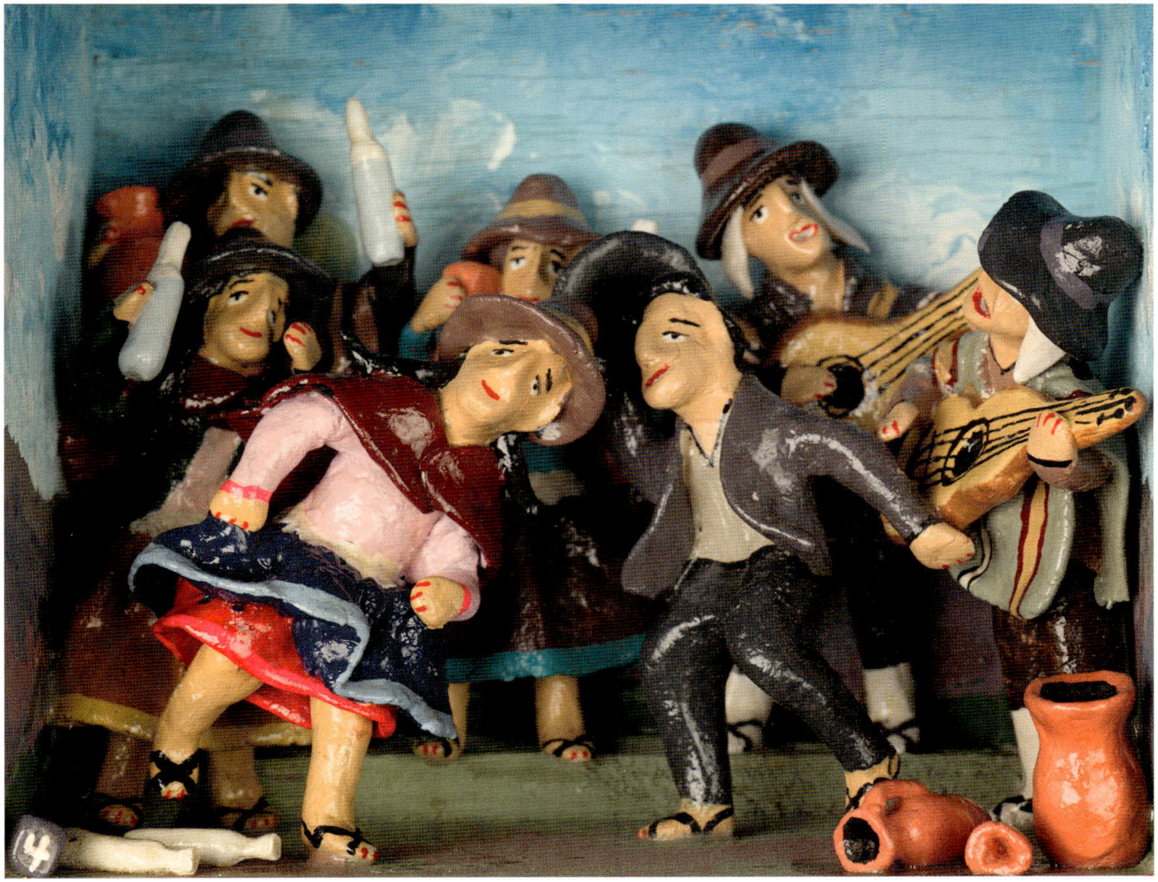

4. TRADITIONAL CUSTOMS: The inhabitants of the Andes have various religious/agro-pastoral festivals. They are generally bohemians and lovers, drink alcohol, and chew the coca leaves. When they sing songs, some interpret the traditional music, producing interesting sounds with their tongues rather than speaking the lyrics of the song. They joyfully dance together in large community celebrations.

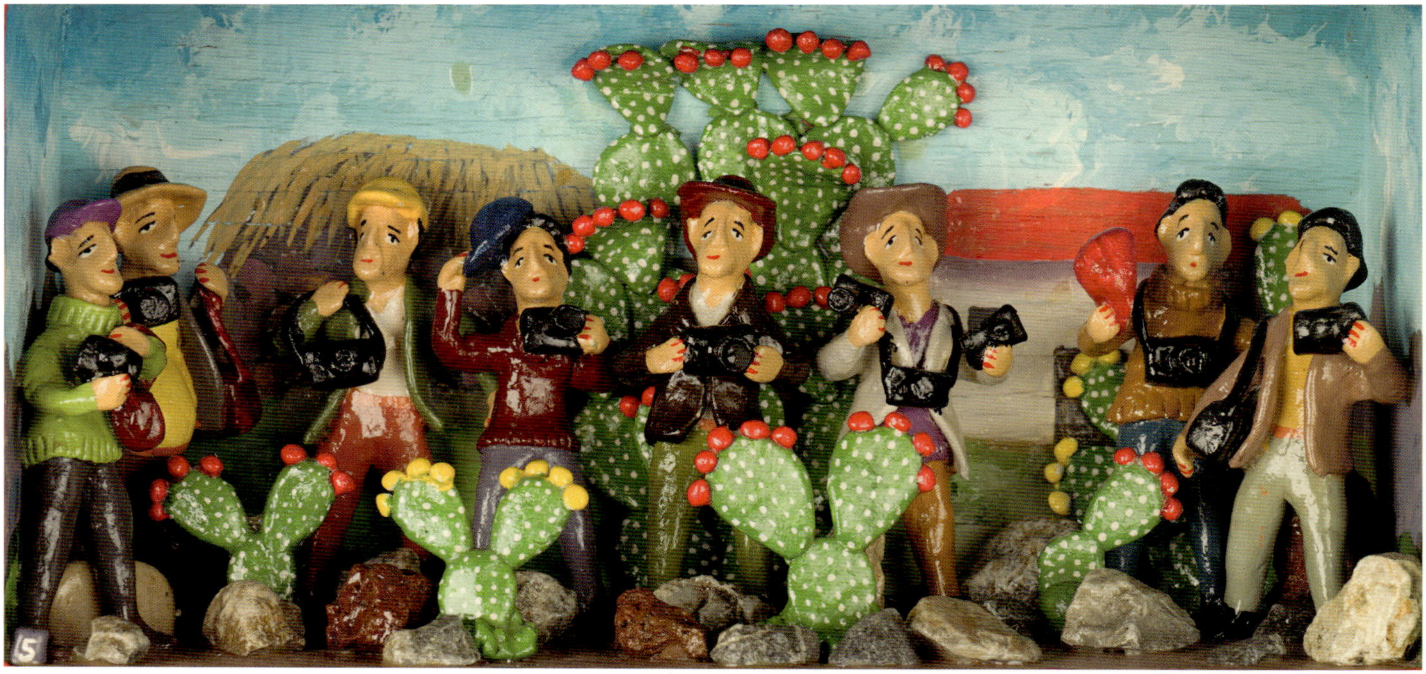

5. THE MARTYRS OF JOURNALISM: The heroic protagonists of this tragic history are eight innocent people with a clear intention to report the truth, only truth, no matter the sacrifice. That is the worthy profession of journalism worldwide. Here they are in the mountain villages of the state of Ayacucho, working with the tools of their trade: cameras, film rolls, bags, backpacks, etc. My friend Octavio is shown among them.

6. REUNION: The reporters gathered in the hostel named Santa Rosa, located near the corner of the Plaza de Armas in Huamanga, Ayacucho. They arranged to go to the scene of the mysterious death of seven people who the military had claimed were members of the Communist group "the Shining Path." The intention of the reporters and their departure date and time were made public information among the people of Huamanga for their own protection.

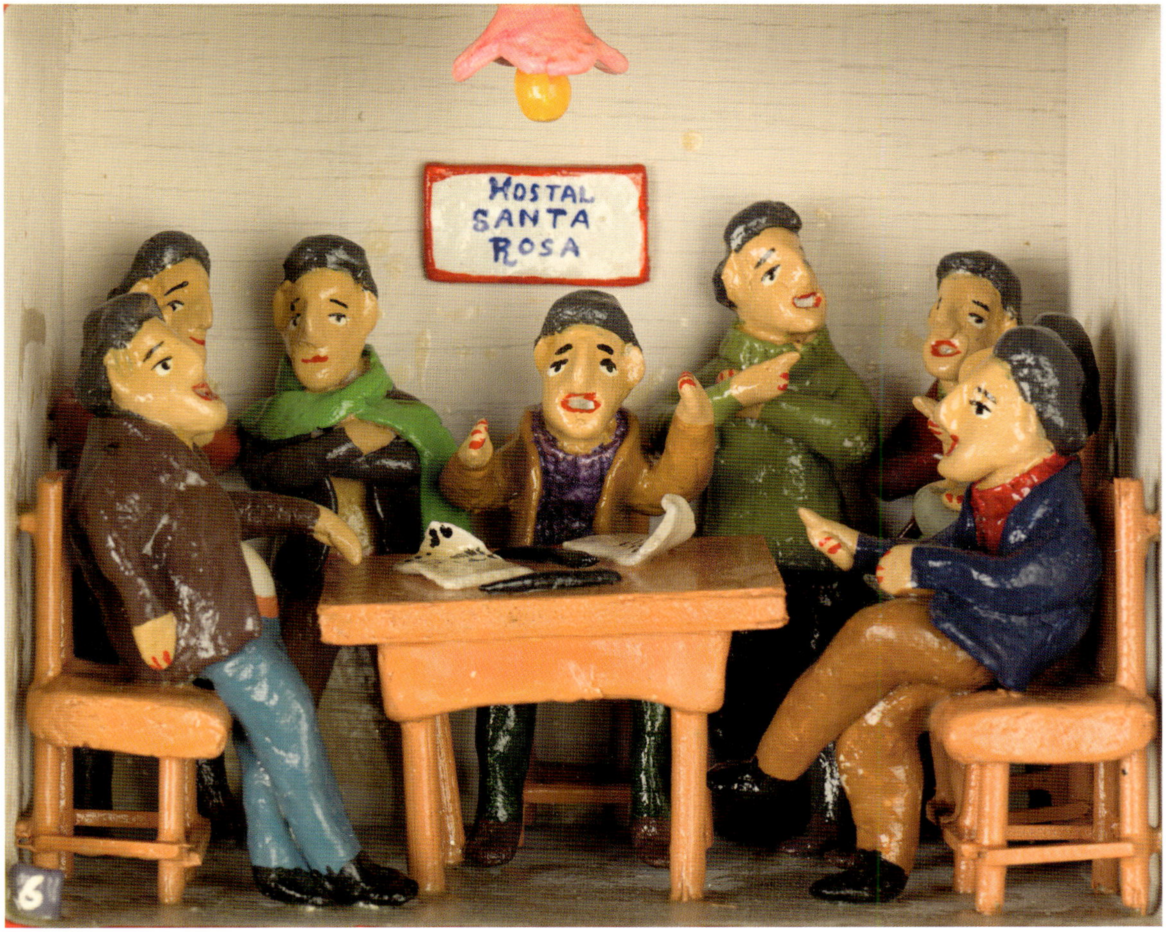

7. MAGDALENA CONTROL POINT: The day after the meeting, the journalists rented a car and drove to the police control point outside the city of Huamanga. There, all the journalists showed their press credentials. The security officers did not ask where they were going, but simply told them to "pass" because they already had been told about their plans.

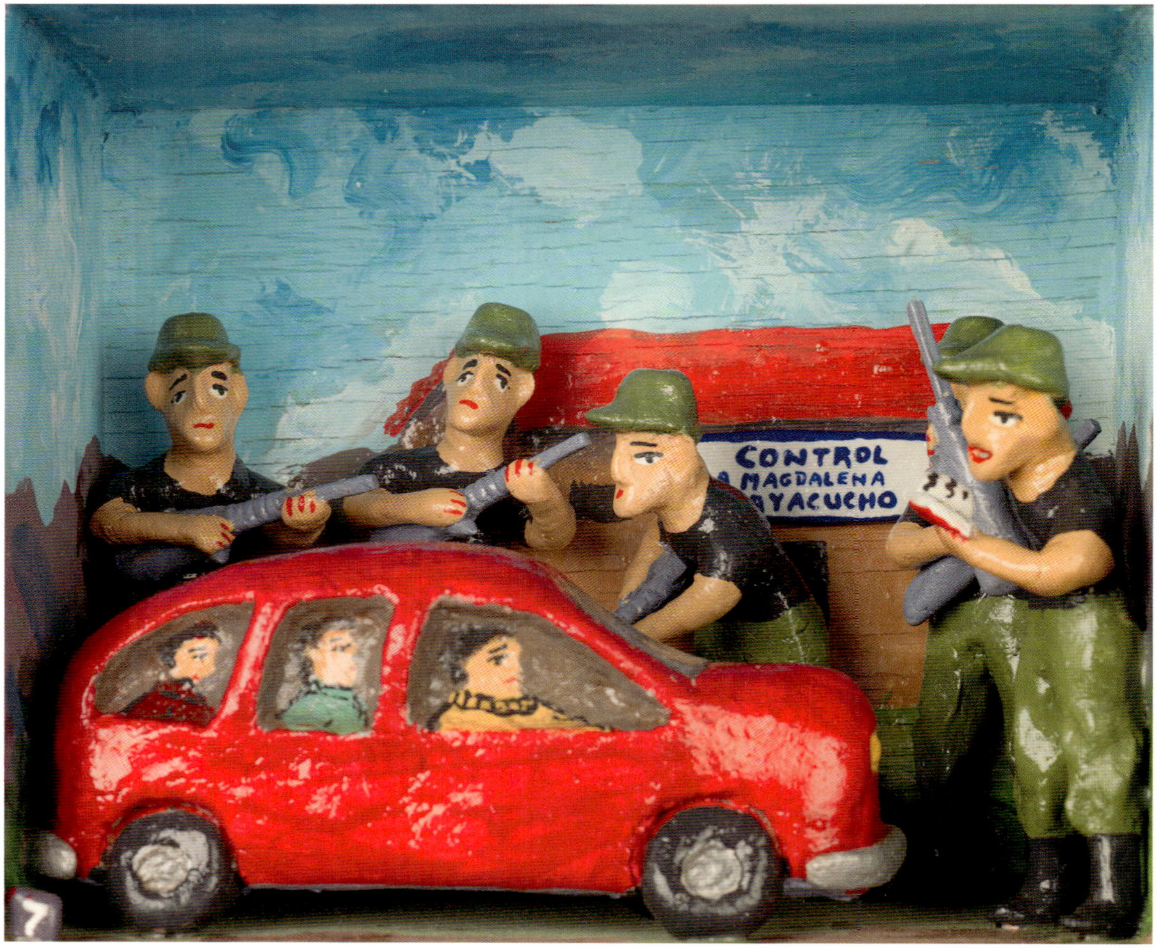

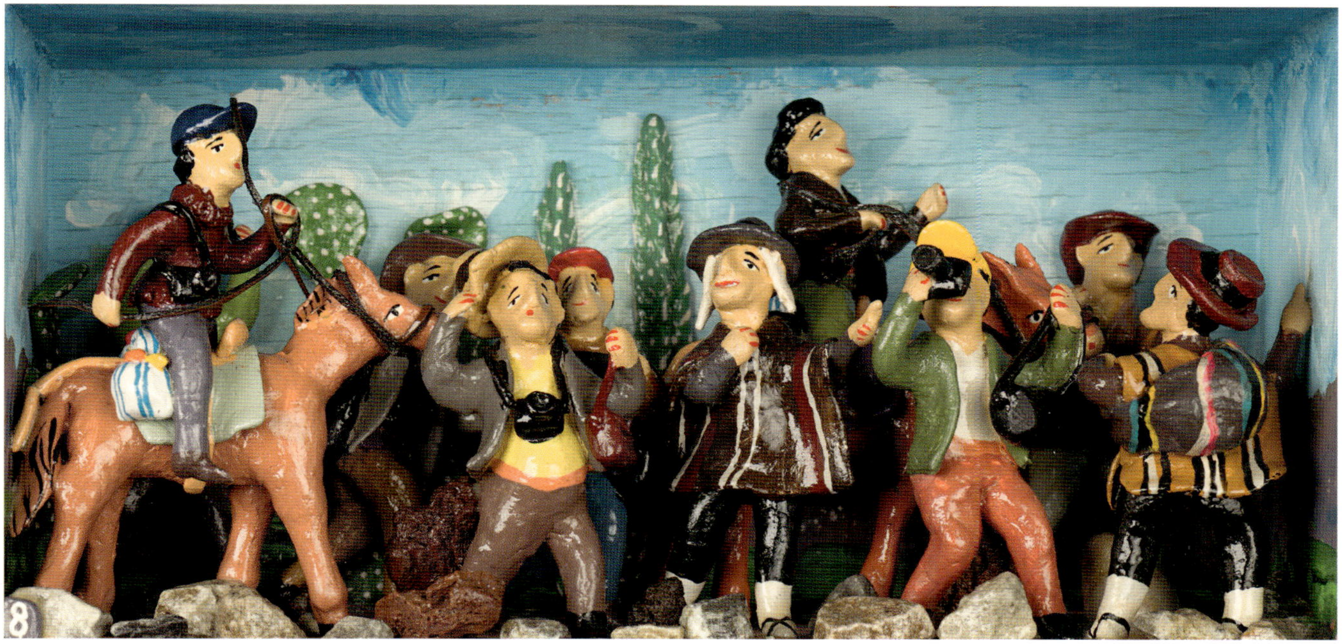

8. ROAD TO HUAYCHAO: After driving several miles, the journalists parked their car and walked or rode on mules or horses guided by two friends of Octavio Infante, who lived in the village of Sachabamba. They traveled over the hills and through the valleys, calculating the time to avoid being caught in the rain or the night.

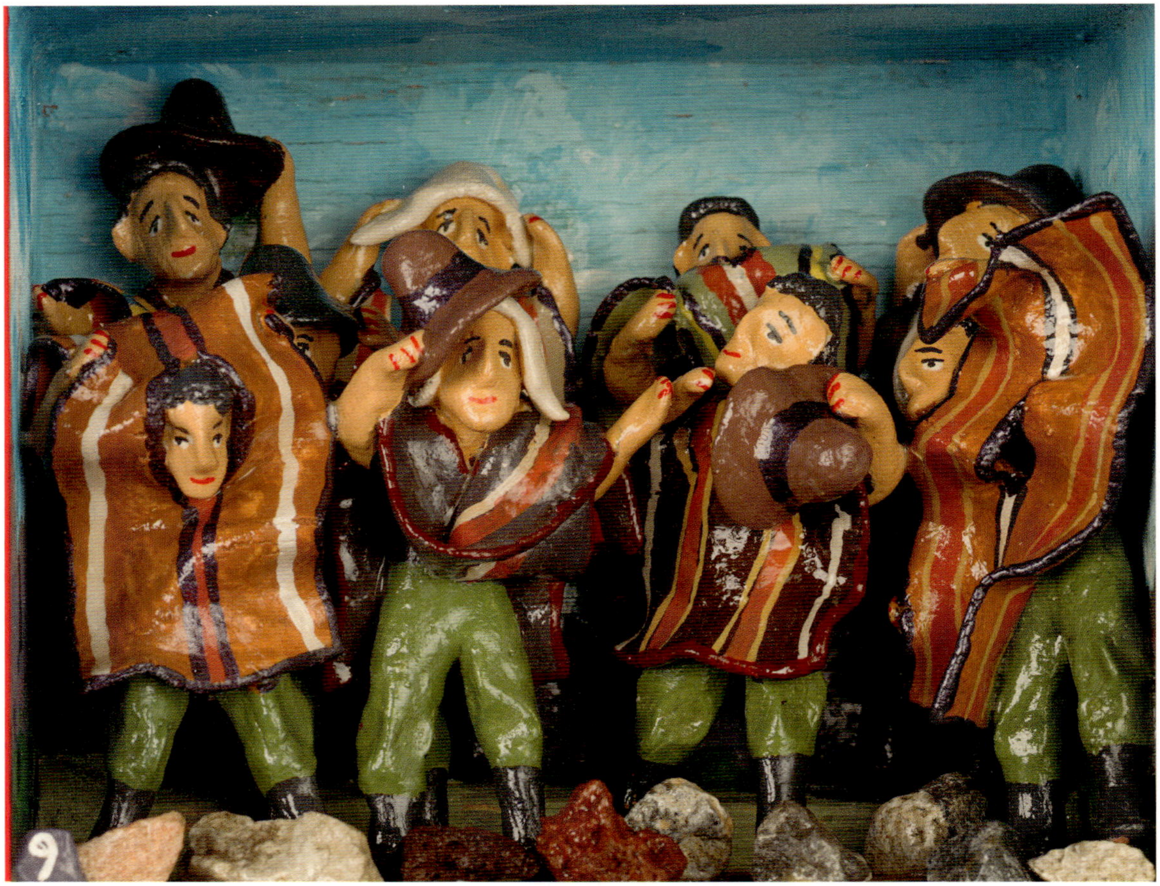

9. DISGUISE: After finding out the true events in the town of Huaychao, the journalists cheerfully and calmly returned. Meanwhile the soldiers who had come by helicopter harassed the villagers of Uchuraccay and instilled fear of the repcrters. Members of the military disguised themselves in the traditional clothing of the villagers.

10. THE BRIBE: The helicopter soldiers provided the commoners of Uchuraccay with a generous amount of food, alcoholic beverages, clothes, cocaine, etc. While they awaited the return of the reporters, they all got drunk together to embolden their courage and lose their fear of killing.

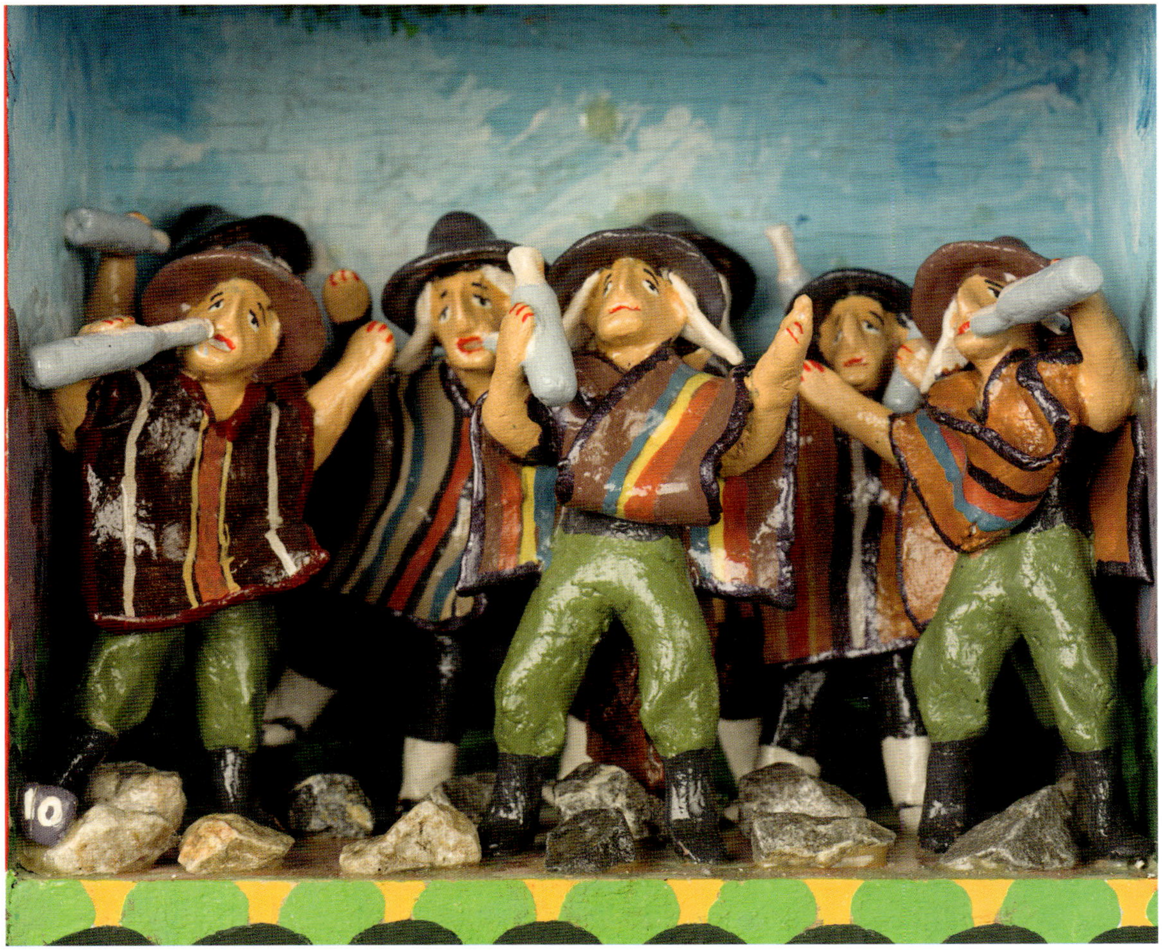

11. THE SLAUGHTER: It was horrible, without mercy, without any words. All the journalists were killed with axes, stones, knives, and machetes. The assassination was a cruel inhumane act, universally condemned by international law.

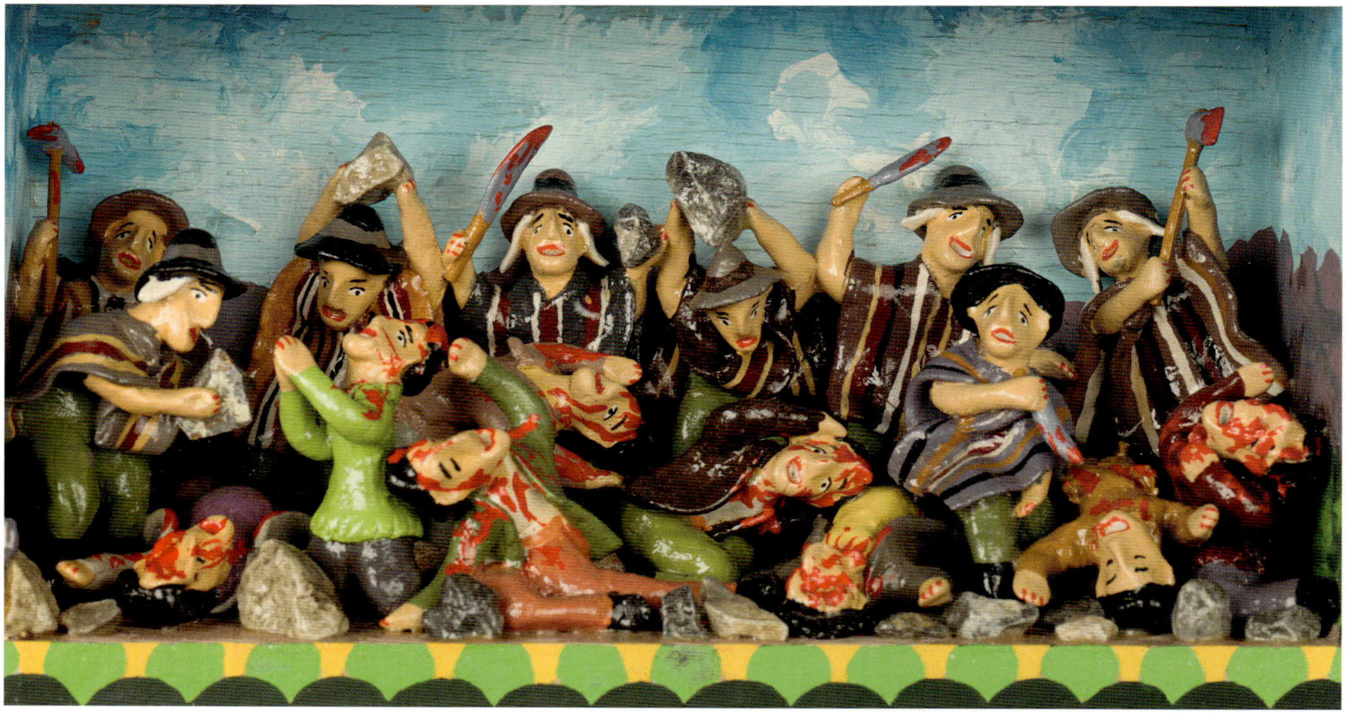

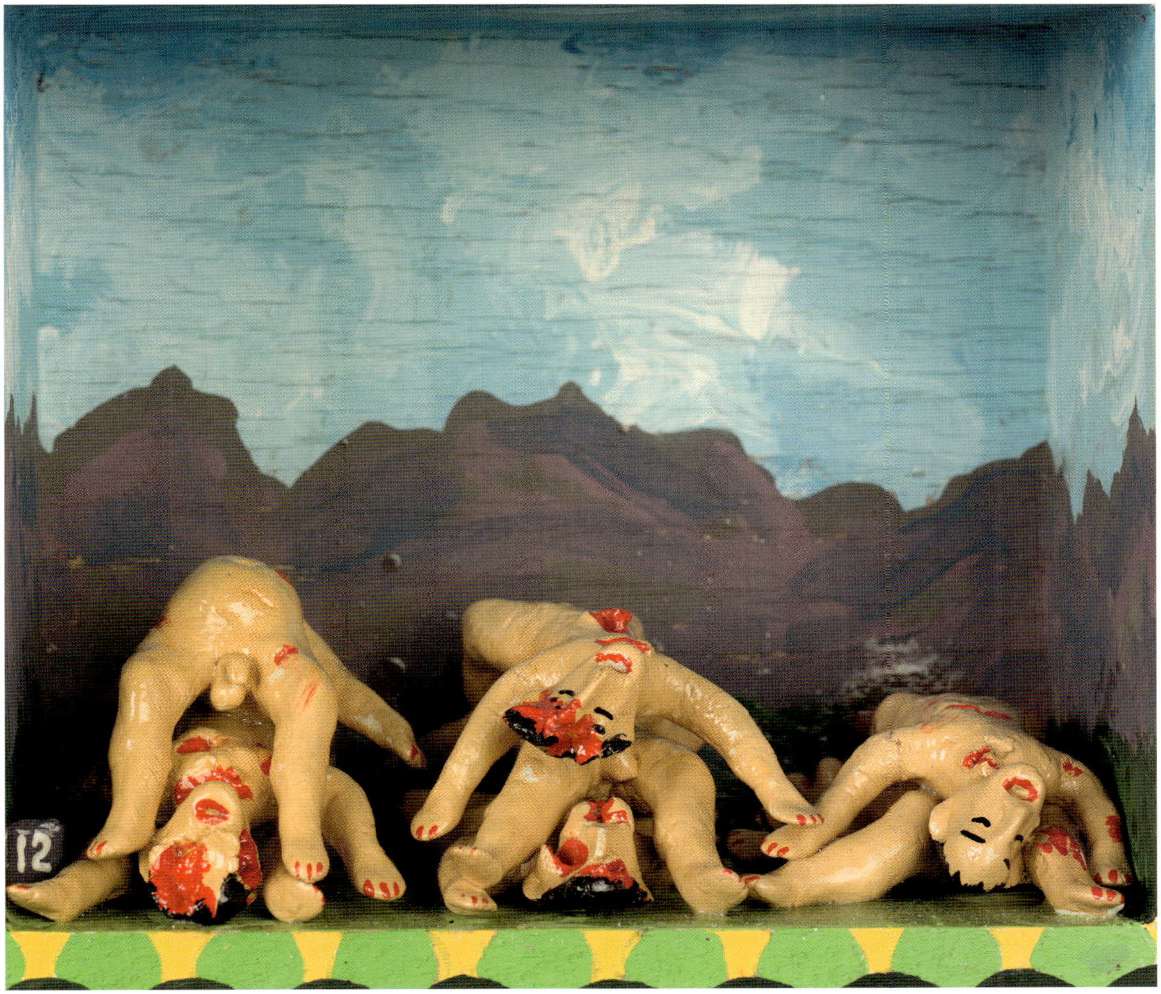

12. THE BURIAL: The bodies of the eight journalists were buried in the village of Uchuraccay, where they were buried in three pits in the ground, superimposed over each other and completely naked, as if they were animals.

Postscript

While completing this book, I spoke often with Jeronimo Lozano. He was always pleased to hear from me, but ultimately he was a man of few words. His English was broken, and he was careful not to overstate his feelings and circumstance. He told stories about his life through his retablos. One of the last times I spoke with him, I was delighted to hear that he'd married Lucy Rickett, who, like him, was a member of the Church of Jesus Christ of Latter-day Saints.

Together, Jeronimo and Lucy found a special happiness, dividing their time between Utah and Pennsylvania, where they stayed on Lucy's family-owned land, once occupied by her McPherson ancestors, in South Gibson, Herrick Township, Susquehanna County, on the north side of Elk Mountain. While there, Jeronimo sometimes created retablo figures of local woodland animals playing bluegrass instruments and placed them on a small base of Pennsylvania bluestone as an homage to his new home.

Jeronimo, in keeping with family tradition, rarely talked about his health and the pulmonary fibrosis he had suffered with for most of his life. When he had to be rushed to the emergency room at the Penn Highland Hospital in Clearfield, all the ICU beds were filled with COVID-19 patients. After three days, on October 2, 2021, Jeronimo died, leaving behind Lucy, the love of his life, and his remaining family: his brother, Edilberto, and Edilberto's son, Percy, as well as his sister, Victoria, and her daughter, Monica, all of whom stayed in frequent contact with him from their homes in Ayacucho, Peru, along with other family members in Lima, Peru, and other areas. Jeronimo was the youngest of twelve children by his mother, Apolinaria Lozano, and his father, Francisco Lozano Quispe. In a *Tribute Archive* obituary, Jeronimo was described as "a gentle, kind man. All who met him were impressed by the spirit he had."

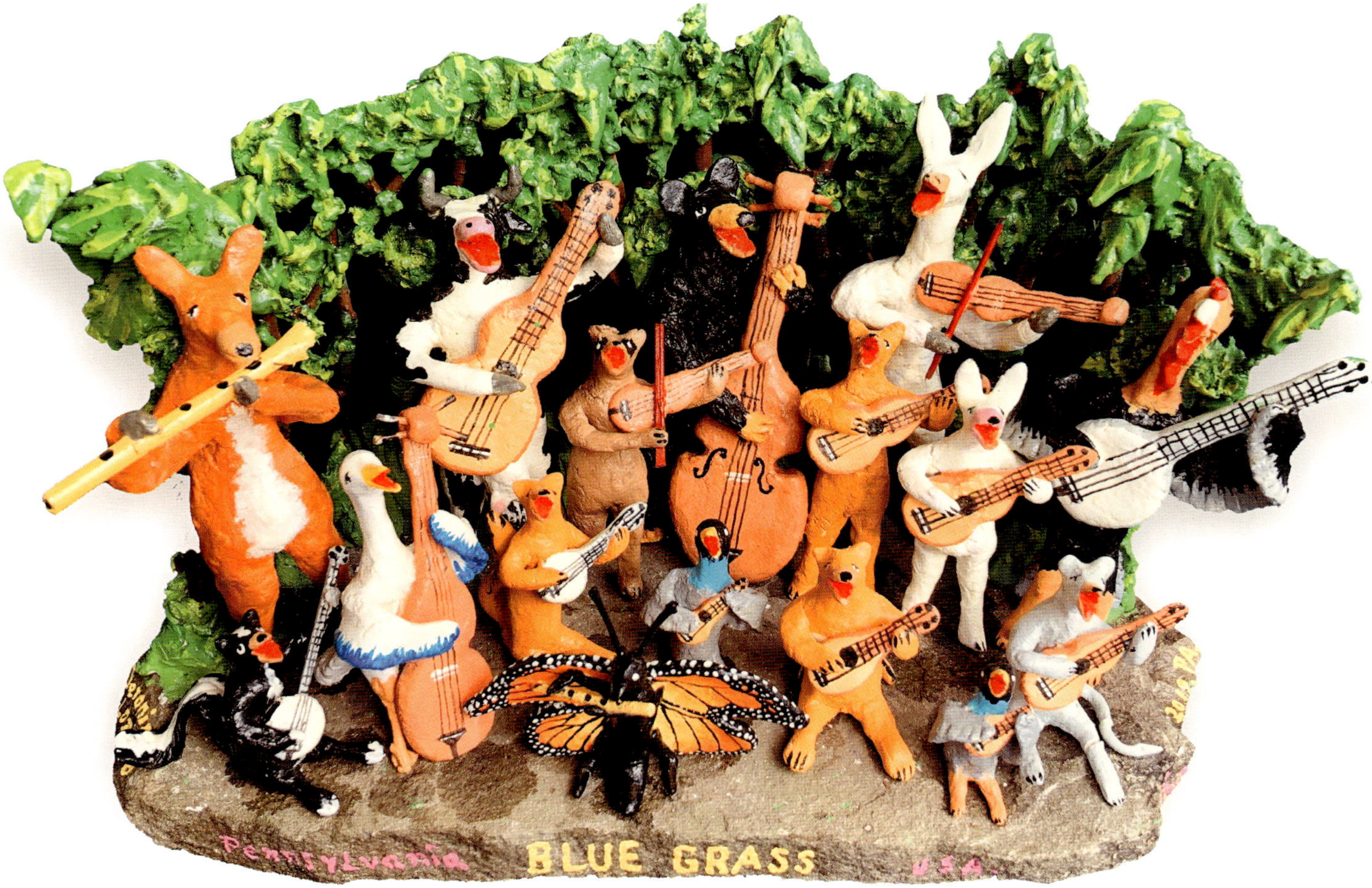

Photograph by Lucy Rickett Lozano

Acknowledgments

Jeronimo Lozano's creativity and perseverance inspired me, from the day I met him in 2008 to his untimely death thirteen years later. His retablos excited me in ways that reconnected me with my endless fascination for toy soldiers and Play-Doh figures I played with as a child. Each of Jeronimo's retablos evoke a sense of wonder, waiting to be discovered.

My wife, Kaleta Doolin, and my family—Alex and Rachel, Breea and Teale, and my granddaughters Emiline and Iris—were always there for me, energizing my work by bringing joy to my life.

Over the years, my work on folk and traditional arts has been supported in part by grants from the National Endowment for the Arts to Documentary Arts, the nonprofit organization I founded in 1985 to advance essential perspectives on historical issues and diverse cultures.

In preparing the manuscript for publication, Kirk Henrichsen was invaluable to me, helping to organize my interview sessions with Jeronimo in Washington, DC, and Salt Lake City, Utah, and he provided translations of the text descriptions accompanying *The Tragedy in Uchuraccay* retablos. Jeronimo's wife, Lucy Rickett Lozano, clarified the chronology of his life. Anthony Hill transcribed my interviews, Kevin Todora and Alan Hatchett made studio photographs of retablos, and Jason Johnson-Spinos assisted me in the editing of my texts, processing photographs, and thinking through the design and organization of this book.

ALAN GOVENAR is an award-winning writer, folklorist, photographer, and filmmaker. He is president of Documentary Arts, a nonprofit organization he founded in 1985 to present essential perspectives on historical issues and diverse cultures. Govenar is a Guggenheim Fellow, the author of over thirty books, and the director of more than two dozen films.

Over the last four decades, Govenar has worked to focus public attention on the recipients of the National Heritage Fellowship, awarded annually by the National Endowment for the Arts. He developed mastersoftraditionalarts.org, which includes biographical entries, photographs, audio recordings, and videos of National Heritage Fellows, with a downloadable education guide that he coauthored with Paddy Bowman and Betty Carter. In addition, he produced and directed two 52-part radio series for national broadcast and the feature-length documentary film Extraordinary Ordinary People. For more information, see documentaryarts.org.

ALSO BY ALAN GOVENAR

NONFICTION

Lightnin' Hopkins: His Life and Blues
Anne Morgan: Photography, Philanthropy and Advocacy (with Mary Niles Maack)
The Blues Come to Texas: Paul Oliver and Mack McCormick's Unfinished Book (with Kip Lornell)
Texas Blues: The Rise of a Contemporary Sound
Untold Glory: African Americans in Pursuit of Freedom, Opportunity and Achievement
The Early Years of Rhythm and Blues
Stoney Knows How: Life as a Sideshow Tattoo Artist
Masters of Traditional Arts: A Biographical Dictionary
African American Frontiers
Portraits of Community
Deep Ellum and Central Track: The Other Side of Dallas (with Jay F. Brakefield)
Ed Hardy: Beyond Skin
Ed Hardy: Art for Life
Meeting the Blues: The Rise of the Texas Sound
Flash from the Past: Classic American Tattoo Designs
A Joyful Noise: A Celebration of New Orleans Music (with Michael P. Smith)
Living Texas Blues

POETRY/FICTION

A Pillow on the Ocean of Time
Boccaccio in the Berkshires
Paradise in the Smallest Thing
Casa di Dante

FOR YOUNG READERS

Extraordinary Ordinary People: Five American Masters of Traditional Arts
Stompin' at the Savoy: The Story of Norma Miller
Osceola: Memories of a Sharecropper's Daughter
Everyday Music

ESSAY COLLECTIONS

Juneteenth Texas: Essays in African-American Folklore (with Francis Abernethy and Patrick B. Mullen)

PLAYS/MUSICALS

Blind Lemon Blues (with Akin Babatunde)
Texas in Paris
Lonesome Blues (with Akin Babatunde)
Stompin' at the Savoy

FILMS

Myth of a Colorblind France
Tattoo Uprising
Extraordinary Ordinary People
You Don't Need Feet to Dance
Serving Second Chances
Master Qi and the Monkey King
The Beat Hotel
Texas Style
The Devil's Swing
The Hard Ride
Cigarette Blues
Stoney Knows How
The Shipwreck of La Belle
Dreams of Conquest
Osceola Mays: Stories, Songs, and Poems